D1420413

International Sales and the Middleman

INTERNATIONAL SALES AND THE MIDDLEMAN

Managing Your Agents and Distributors

John P. Griffin

MERCURY

Copyright © John P. Griffin, 1990

First published in 1990
by Mercury Books
Gold Arrow Publications Limited
862 Garratt Lane, London SW17 0NB

Set in Linotron Bembo by
Phoenix Photosetting, Chatham, Kent
Printed and bound in Great Britain by
Mackays of Chatham PLC, Chatham, Kent

British Library Cataloguing in Publication Data

Griffin, John P.
  International sales and the middleman.
  1. Great Britain. Business firms. Sales management
  I. Title
  658.8100941

  ISBN 1–85251–049–8

CONTENTS

ACKNOWLEDGEMENTS

All my thanks to Anne, Mark, John, Luke and Matthew for all their enthusiasm and encouragement; to Dr Jack Fitzpatrick for his technical support; and to Joseph, Noel and Brian Griffin for their very special assistance.

INTRODUCTION

It is hard to come across good definitions of what is meant by 'marketing'. Most of them are unintelligible. I remember recently reading an article on export marketing by an academic. He started his piece with three individual definitions. None could be understood. The article concluded as it had begun – leaving the reader ignorant, but in awe.

Definitions anyhow are boring. Descriptions are better. And *Chambers* briefly and delightfully describes marketing as the aggregate of functions in getting goods from the producer to the consumer. Just that.

Of all the various functions which come into play in getting a product to its target, channel selection and management must surely be one of the most crucial. It is hard to think of many significant industries or companies where intermediaries do not play a major role in the distribution chain. Of course, there are some. For instance, Mrs Brown who produces eggs in low and seasonal quantities will probably only sell directly to her coterie of approved neighbours. Other producers of highly specialised products in highly accessible markets may also be able to eliminate middlemen. Thus in America there are some excellent examples of industries in specialised consumer products, such as wood-burning stoves, specialty household tools, leisure accessories and varieties of craft items, where the size and homogeneity of the market allows a direct marketing exercise through a company's own catalogues and advertising. Others have become so mammoth, notably in fast food retailing, that they have dispensed altogether with independent intermediaries. Others again, such as aeroplane manufacturers, have such a compact international customer base that go-betweens are rarely necessary other than for political reasons.

The vast majority of producers, however, sooner or later in the development of their business either deploy or fall prey to middlemen – depending on their perspective. For example, most consumer goods go through retailers for access to the public at large. And the retail networks themselves will often access the supplier through an intermediary wholesaler. Other manufacturers may take on many of the consumers directly but still rely on specialised distributors to reach very specialised customer groups. And the role of intermediary, or distributor, really comes into its own in reaching customers in markets and geographical areas where the producer cannot operate economically. In fact the use or otherwise of intermediaries is nearly always the result of a fairly simple mathematical calculation. All the possible permutations of sales levels, prices, selling costs and dealer margins are thrown into a big cauldron and stirred about until just the right mixture sets for profitability and strategic comfort. In the vast number of cases the emerging formula will involve distributors or agents in accessing at least some, and often all, of one's markets.

In domestic and international markets, then, the role of intermediaries, or middlemen, is practically indispensable. Their management is clearly critical in bringing a product to a market and keeping it there. Yet an afternoon in the library or a poll of marketing graduates, young and old, will confirm that this subject, distribution management, gets relatively little attention. The focus is usually on cost studies, statistical analysis, the market mix, media, promotion and arrays of consumer studies and case histories. Channel selection and management is usually relegated to a few paragraphs or a passing comment.

For this reason, recruiting marketing graduates is generally a nightmare. They can trot out the elements of marketing *ad nauseam*, but rarely have any idea where to begin in the practical business of ramping up sales through distributor networks. Their ultimate challenge will probably be to mobilise others, the famous middlemen, to do their jobs for them – yet their courses and books deal little with the key challenge of motivating and manipulating distribution networks. It seems as though the skills and tricks involved are consigned to be passed on by oral tradition or to be painfully and more commonly learned through bitter frustration and failure.

International sales and export development, especially, calls for new dimensions in technique and maturity in cultivating distributor networks. In fact the art of channel selection and management is so critical in international business for all companies, big and small, that it arguably transcends all those other elements more commonly prioritised and which are canted regularly in journals and texts. Most articles on building exports lead with 'getting the product right' and labour test marketing, consumer studies, pricing, packaging, promotion, advertising, exhibiting, forecasting and so forth. Selecting, managing and motivating distribution networks will mostly occupy only a few paragraphs, and will underwhelm the reader with such counsel as 'choose good distributors' and other hints in the use of state agencies, commerce departments and industry associations in sussing out 'reliable' importers and agents!

This type of emphasis has to be misplaced. It does not satisfactorily address those millions of products which seem to fit all the academic market criteria but never get to see the light of day on the international marketplace. Neither does it address the case of the passable and marginally competitive 'me too' products which outrun their competitors world-wide. Usually, and paradoxically, the ingredient which makes the difference is a deep understanding of the psychology and technique of distribution management.

To sum up – there is too much emphasis on the consumer and the product and too much focus on selling to users. In fact a user's preference is only one factor in determining a purchase – and often a minor one. The weight and the quality of a distributor's effort in bringing the product to a market, and the way in which he handles consumers, are often the deciding issues in export success. Put another way: between manufacturers and consumers there is a vast and largely indispensable array of intermediaries, middlemen, primary customers – call them what you will. We need to devote as much time and energy to selling these groups as we do to the craft of persuading consumers.

This book therefore concentrates on channel, not product. It should therefore be unlike anything yet written. Certainly no references are quoted, because none were used. It is not an attack on current marketing theory or college courses but rather, and hopefully, a supplement to them. It sets out on the business of building an international business from absolute scratch and from the clear perspective that the real challenges lie in mobilising intermediaries.

Certain assumptions are made so that we can focus on the step-by-step creation of export business. We assume that the product has proven itself domestically and exhibits at least some potential in overseas markets. Alternatively the product may be entirely new but well researched in terms of international competitiveness. Compatibility with overseas safety standards, norms and tastes is taken for granted.

Some obvious exceptions to our strategy are overlooked, starting with those types of companies, already mentioned, who can side-step intermediaries altogether. We also ignore those companies which are in a position to bypass most intermediary complexities by signing global franchises with existing international merchandising companies. Nor do we talk about companies, typically in the pharmaceutical business, which are big enough and experienced enough in domestic markets to invest megabucks and take short cuts in getting to their customers overseas. Many of the issues we address are relevant to any type of export operation, but they are easier and more logical to deal with in the context of growing an international business from the very beginning.

When we use the term 'distributor' we refer to independent companies who take ownership of merchandise themselves and deploy sales and marketing skills, to a greater or lesser extent, in passing the goods down the distribution chain. Many of the same principles apply, however, in selecting and managing manufacturers' representatives or 'agents' who perform many of the same services without actually purchasing the merchandise.

This book has been written for those involved in building an international business, or those who plan on doing that sort of thing for a living. It is also designed for anyone who has tried but failed. So many times we have a really super product which tests well and should be a flyer but the sales just don't materialise – at least not fast enough to keep the bank manager off the doorstep!

There is so much fool's gold, so many easy solutions, so many misapprehensions. Over and over, government export boards, departments of commerce, export trading houses and tribes of duplicitous dealers are taken as the Holy Grail, and fledgeling export businesses fail even before the ink dries.

Maybe your international business is growing reasonably well but slower than your industry peers'? Are there curious black-spots on your export map where, for one reason or another, you never seem to have any luck? Perhaps you've been cloistered for three years in a marketing school but, like a tree hidden in a forest, you just can't quite visualise – between the endless lists, summaries and equations – how to buy sand for a dollar and sell it to the Arabs for two! Or maybe you're a production engineer or an accountant who wants to try to understand those crazy export people. Most people in a company easily understand naïve international staff but rarely trust or relate to the ones who really know what they're doing. You may be, yourself, a distributor, an agent, a wholesaler or a retailer who needs to understand and protect himself – at least from those suppliers who know what they're about! Hopefully you will see in this book a blend of psychologies in dealings with intermediaries which will appeal to anyone in the business of buying, or selling. And who is not?

The book draws on experience and success in international selling. But it certainly does not have all the answers. It tries to concentrate on those psychological and practical fundamentals which will get an international market entrant out of adolescence as quickly as possible and on to basics in moving product through distributors. But even these skills will be useless with the wrong attitude. If you come across to your customers as ugly, bombastic, bullying, treacherous or insincere, then this, or any book, will be of little value.

Finally, some readers may find the book often hard-nosed and cynical. Others will recognise the big and often ugly world of international selling as they know it. And a keen if not cynical sense of humour has always been a vital antidote to the rigours of global wheeling and dealing!

1

FUNDAMENTALS

This book revolves on middlemen, intermediaries, third parties. There are some pretty shocking keys in manipulating these people. These fundamentals need to be understood right away and to achieve that – we need to start at the middle!

Let's just assume for a minute that you've done the homework. The territory has been analysed. You have chosen a suitable distribution mechanism. You have profiled and screened various distribution companies that might fit into your scheme of things – and you've made your selection and contracted with a distributor, or group of distributors.

You have just established a relationship. It may be destined to be short-lived – or it might transpire to be one of the longest and proudest of your career. Whether long or short, to be successful it must have, at its root, equilibrium.

Balance

The most basic and essential motivation for a distributor is profit. Sales volumes, technology, sales support, product training, fabulous product literature – all of these are worthless if he doesn't, at the end of the day, make money. And the moneymaking has to be balanced. No relationship will last where the dealer is making a 45 per cent gross margin but where the supplier has been pared back to factory cost to keep the product competitive in his marketplace. The relationship must be profitable for both.

Stemming from agreement for mutual and balanced profits will flow a balance in all areas of the commercial relationship. This is illustrated by a story about a dentist who was dealing with a really nervous patient. The poor patient crouched in the hot seat while the dentist advanced on him with a particularly sharp and vicious-looking tool. As the dentist reached the chair the victim's right hand shot out and deftly grasped the dentist in a specially sensitive area. Still clutching firmly, the patient relaxed into the chair. 'Now then,' he said to the dentist, 'let's not hurt each other . . .' The essence of balance in a relationship!

A Fair Share?

Another key fundamental is a clear understanding of your true task with a distributor. Even experienced international businessmen get this one wrong! Most people when asked what their key goal is with a distributor will talk about 'increasing sales', or 'expanding market share' or other similar abstracts.

You will have chosen to go through a distributor because either the entry costs of a direct selling organisation are too high or because, and more likely, the level of available business is not high enough to fund a direct selling effort within a reasonable time period. Herein lies the *raison d'être* for distribution companies. By sharing their resources among a number of principals, they generate enough sales volume to drive a business profitably. Here, of course, also lies the weakness of distributor organisations. They are polygamous. Rather than concentrating on your products, distributor sales staff carry many 'lines' and ration their selling time out on the different products either as their instinct dictates or as directed by sales management.

One's primary goal therefore with distributors can be simply stated: it is to fight for an unfair share of distributor sales time. It is to take their sales force, marketing and sales management and to motivate, cajole, bully, threaten, seduce and compromise them so as to take time from other products and have it devoted to yours. It is a reasonable goal and not a cynical one. Provided all other factors are kept in balance – primarily profits – then you are not rendering the distributor a disservice. You are merely ensuring that his company is making profit with your products and not with someone else's. His company and his sales team represent a certain finite resource, not unlike a motor engine with a fixed power output. Provided all other strategic elements are in balance, the distributor will care little about the source of the profit or the fact that your product is commanding a quarter of his engine capacity rather than some other.

The Real Competitor

I cannot overstress the importance of this key issue of share of distributor resource. Invariably, looking for growth, pressurised international sales managers focus on competitors, price comparisons, technical issues, publicity and so forth. In fact the first area for analysis should be the available extra resource from his distribution group. In reality his biggest competitor is not the German or Japanese company making a similar product, but rather all those other completely unrelated products being touted around by distributor sales staff. For example, a surgical instrument supplier may perceive his problem as being an aggressive East German scissors maker whereas, in reality, he is losing out to a bandage manufacturer who has found a better way to command the attention of the same dealer's sales team.

The Black Widow Syndrome

Yet another fundamental, and one which is essential to grasp early in the game, is that distributors, like horse-traders and second-hand car salesmen, have been given a special dispensation to use lies and deception as a daily tool of their trade and yet retain a mantle of respectability and integrity in their business community. The horse and car dealers can justify this on the quite reasonable assumption that no one would buy either of those products if he were fully *au fait* with their past histories.

Distributors have a similar rationale. They realise that from the moment intercourse starts with a principal, it is in reality a black widow situation. They understand that success with a principal's products carries a paradoxical risk of termination, which will occur at the point where sales have risen to a level sufficient to sustain a direct selling effort by the principal. This then is the Armageddon which faces all intermediaries, or distributors. To pretend it doesn't exist or that it will go away is foolish. That would be to deny the most basic of business principles. No, all but the most naïve distributors know and understand this point, and the cleverest and most successful are those who stretch the distributor's useful life cycle to the maximum.

This point is worth labouring. Let's say that a manufacturer of self-cleaning lavatory seats is planning sales in the Danish market. After a reasonable period of study he decides on certain initial sales targets which he can plan with reasonable confidence. Having checked competitors' prices, and knowing his own costs, he concludes that there would be a 40 per cent gross margin available to fund the Danish sales effort. In other words, the cost to put the seats in his Copenhagen warehouse would be £60 each and they could be sold competitively for the equivalent of £100 in local currency. So far, so good. However, the seat-maker cannot confidently predict sales of more than 5,000 seats a year, at least initially. This would yield no more than £200,000 a year to run the Danish sales operation – clearly an inadequate amount to provide national sales representation, run an office, and provide secretarial and dispatch services together with national advertising, trade shows and the like. So he will be driven into a commercial relationship with an independent Danish distributor who has a national sales force, offices, ware-house and all the other necessary resources to market the seats throughout Denmark. The Danish distributor can live with a sales target of only 5,000 seats a year because he also sells paper dispensers, liquid soap dispensers and a wide range of other complementary products targeted at roughly the same market. So a beautiful but tenuous relationship is born.

The seat manufacturer soon realises that while the distributor has a national sales force of ten which should, in theory, give excellent coverage, their time in practice is torn between the other sixty-odd lines they have to represent. The seat manufacturer soon realises that two of his own dedicated salesmen would be better than twenty of the dealer's. He dreams of the day when sales may grow to the point where he can confidently fund his own direct sales operation in Denmark.

The Mushroom Treatment

The distributor has, of course, realised this threat from the moment the deal was conceived. For him the challenge is to sell enough to encourage the seat-maker, and to keep the franchise, but not so much as to tempt him!

A variety of other tactics are employed to protect the franchise, the principal one being the legendary mushroom treatment – an expression drawn from the practice of farming these delicacies by keeping them in the dark and feeding them practically exclusively on manure! Put another way, the less a supplier knows about a market the more indispensable will be the distributor. As the distributor sees it, the best way to protect a franchise is through dependence, and the best way to fuel dependence is through fear. Fear of the unknown – by starving the supplier of data. And fear of perceived but illusory dangers which the dealer has created in the mind of the supplier through a variety of techniques, all usually based on concealment of the truth and, periodically, on downright lies.

The essential challenge, therefore, in manipulating an international distributor network is to master the following three fundamentals.

At the highest level your distributor managers must perceive the relationship as being at least equally profitable to any other franchise, and hopefully even more profitable. Your control over, or clout with, the distributor will be directly related to the contribution of your products to profits. The skill lies in maximising his profits, keeping them in balance with your own, and all the while maintaining competitiveness and increasing market share.

The distributor sales team must be seen as a resource for which he who fights hardest will command most. In fact the greater part of this book is devoted to ways and means of persuading dealer sales staff to spend more and more of their time on your products.

Finally, there must be the realisation that information and opinions provided by distributors must be largely discounted in compiling a database. His goals are not your goals, his ways cannot be yours.

Motivating proprietors of distribution companies by stretching their profits, seducing their sales teams and the daily Confucian battle with half-truths and distortions, bluff and counter-bluff – these are the paramount daily challenges of international business managers.

Foul But Fair

Of course there will be some who will be appalled by such an apparently cynical approach – theorists and so forth, who talk the language of 'partnership' between dealer and principal. They point to the benefits of open exchange of data, to the early admission of mutual vulnerability, to 'understanding' and 'trust'. When interviewing candidates for international sales I watch carefully for signs of such deep-rooted naïvety, as it will certainly represent an appalling handicap to any aspirant to international sales success. The goals of suppliers and distributors are divergent. It is this inalienable fact that precludes trust. Because this point has been well understood by the business community, globally, much expense and effort has been devoted to trying to conceal it. One corporate brochure after another labours the 'trust' and 'partnership' element – really to the point of Freudian admission. In truth, they really protest too much. I've worked on both sides of the fence. Today, as a supplier, if there's one thing which sparks all my senses into a full-scale red alert it is some toadying distributor crouched in front of me like an adder, voice dropped to a coarse whisper, saying: 'I want to be blunt and honest and open and frank with you . . . very confidentially . . . off the record . . .'

Odds on he's building up to the lie of the month!

2

ANALYSIS

Before you start anything you need a gameplan, which will need a certain amount of research and study to carry any value. But I want to emphasise that any gameplan is better than none. Europe is such a big place, 330 million if you include Eastern Europe. Study of such a vast market prior to entry often proves such a daunting task that the whole programme can get into a state of frozen funk with no real plan materialising. Don't laugh, this is a very frequent psychological phenomenon. It's often very well hidden under a mountain of intelligent-sounding fears, concerns and apparent barriers. It's difficult to detect, because the individual charged with doing the research has a monopoly on much of the data. He is not consciously aware of his problem but has access to a lot of objections once his subconscious has, out of fear, rejected the whole proposition. There are less subtle cases where someone will want to deliberately obstruct an international programme. Maybe it will involve unwelcome additional travel or just excessive responsibility for the individual concerned. And of course there is always the fear of failure.

It is a strange but relevant fact that 'exporting' or 'international business' often carries an emphasis and hype that far exceeds its relevance, creating imbalances in time and effort within companies. It's not uncommon to find a national manager responsible for 70 million dollars' worth of domestic business devoting over 30 per cent of his time and attention to an export market currently worth 3 million. Exports are glamorous, heavily emphasised by governments, prestigious for companies and high profile within an organisation. An export programme is something no smart executive would wish to fall down on – this fear of failure will often exhibit itself in an attitude of negativism and procrastination in getting going with a programme.

Get Rolling

Any programme is a thousand times better than none. Also, what is really needed to get the ball rolling initially is not an excellent plan, or even a very good one – just a reasonable plan. The real data, and the solid market information, will not emerge from the planning phase. It will emerge from experience. Therefore the sooner one gets going with a programme, almost any programme, the better.

The same principle will emerge when it comes to distributor selection. When you're starting from ground zero, and provided you have taken the right moves to contractually protect yourself, almost any distributor, or distribution arrangement, is better than none.

As we've stated, this book is primarily for those setting up an indirect representation and sales network. Also we've agreed that the principles don't vary significantly whether you are using a distributor or a manufacturer's representative, or agent.

Representation and Supply

Either way, when you are at your desk wondering where to go next, don't spend too long on planning, statistical studies, industry reports, technical press, demographics and so forth. Your first and foremost need in any market will be representation. That is to say that somehow, by hook or by crook, you've got to get people out into the market showing your products, exhibiting them, tendering them, advertising them, making the calls. Until this happens all is theory, and of course the most crucial point is that until this happens you won't have any sales!

The next need will be supply of the product – assuming some

can be sold! In other words, at around the same time that the product gets representation you'll need to be arranging for its physical distribution – or simply a way to get the product from your factory in Palo Alto to the final customer in Aarhuis.

The element of study and preparation prior to launching a product in an overseas market, or before making a change in distribution, will change and grow enormously as time goes on and you become more mature in the market. For now, just remember you want to get cracking on the business of building an incremental market for existing successful home-market products. And for this purpose the all-important priority is representation and supply. Stocking distributors will, in the vast majority of situations, provide both of these elements. And if you want to get going quickly, get your feet wet and really start learning about how the market in Thailand, Japan or Belgium ticks, then set about getting distributors as quickly as possible – not great ones, not even very good ones, just acceptable distributors.

Choose and Grade

The first thing you will have to do is choose those countries you want to attack and prioritise them. Here again, libraries and statistical analysis can be very dangerous. There are the obvious pitfalls, for example the study of populations. Mainland China, as we all know, has over a billion people and represents a mouth-watering statistical study for practically any business. The point, of course, is that it is a poor country by Western standards and has very low reserves of foreign currency. Hence most of its foreign purchasing is necessarily focused on strategic imports, high technology, medical and so forth.

At the height of the Shah's reign, Iran was an excellent market for a wide variety of modern Western products in electronics, healthcare and the like. Recently, as a war zone, it was a poor bet, with foreign currencies being soaked up by the war effort and many foreign countries banned as suppliers for political reasons. At the same time black-lists disappeared and currencies surfaced quickly for key strategic imports – so judgement is needed.

A preparation for the treatment of bowel disorders might be a flyer in the United Kingdom, where there is an extremely high rate of disease of the colon, but a non-runner in Japan, where diseases of the lower gastrointestinal tract are relatively rare.

If you are a specialised manufacturer of a component used in the fabrication of computer keyboards then a relatively large number of countries can be scratched off your list, as you will be interested only in countries with a significant OEM (own equipment manufacturer) base.

Some places are going to be just too difficult or too expensive to get to for the potential rewards. Iceland represents a sophisticated society with needs for practically all those items enjoyed by advanced European countries. With a population of only 205,000, however, it will be difficult to generate enough sales to pay for a lot of visits or in-market work, and difficult also to motivate a dealer in Iceland to dedicate a lot of effort to any individual product line!

Some countries appear to have all the right 'readings' – West Germany, for example. The statistics are so exciting that many a priority study ends here. Over 60 million people; an extremely wealthy country; an enormous consumer market demanding the latest and best in electronics and every kind of high-technology gadget and convenience; highly stable politically; mouth-watering economic indicators; one of the finest infrastructures in the world.

All this is true, and yet the German market is accepted as one of the most difficult, if lucrative, to break into. Brand recognition and trust are major elements not quickly gained. There are regulatory mountains to be negotiated. There is intense loyalty to established brands. There are exacting standards for the quality, content and relevance of sales support materials.

France is a similar case in question, with a formidable population, a fantastic infrastructure, and a huge demand for sophisticated products in industry, electronics, medicine, agriculture and so on. Yet the French loyalty to domestic products is intense and the measures they have employed to protect themselves against imports are legendary. Thus the French market represents a tremendous opportunity for high-technology products not locally produced, but an extremely difficult and expensive market in challenge for a product which faces established domestic French competition.

The Trading Culture

There is the often anomalous question of the quality of the nationally available distribution culture. For one historical reason or another there may be a poor overall standard in available distribution outlets. The United States is a classic example. Here is a truly vast market of some 250 million people, an extraordinarily wealthy country with enormous economic strength and stability. It is extremely stable politically. It has an enormous consumer mentality, with the major element of its economy sustained internally. It is both producer and consumer of the very latest in high-technology equipment. Most significant of all for a potential market entrant is the fact that, even with its size, it is homogeneous – uniform currency, no borders, highly efficient pan-American transportation, universally envied communications systems, and uniform and effective laws governing trading, pricing and so forth. Finally, it has a liberal and relatively fair attitude towards imports and competition in general. Principally arising from its homogeneity and its size, therefore, most producers of high-technology equipment quickly reach, or alternatively can confidently quickly predict, a high enough level of sales to support a direct selling operation – and of course a direct selling operation is always infinitely preferable, if it can be sustained, in increasing market share and controlling markets. Therefore, because most successful high-technology producers eventually go direct, US distribution houses have evolved into a sort of lower order than their Asian or European counterparts, being relegated to products of lower technical content, consumables and so forth. Their counterparts in Australia, Malaysia or Italy will, however, have evolved differently. Although these markets can be lucrative, direct entry is less frequently profitable and distribution houses will consequently have evolved to meet the requirements for distributing more sophisticated equipment. They will have the necessary specialised staff, technical service resources, and so on. So a handle on the general quality of the distribution culture is essential.

The Joker

There will be another paradoxical factor, a wild card in the priority grading of your target markets. Distribution companies are, in the final analysis, made up of people. And people, as we know, are far from being predictable, homogeneous or consistently reasonable. Time and again you can present a dealer with the Holy Grail of products for his market – competitive price, better quality, faster deliveries, excellent margin, all the textbook ingredients for better sales – but with no result. This will often happen because some highly important but abstract motives are missing. These are usually questions of relationship: the personal relationship between the owner of the distribution company and the owner of the supply company, the relationship between the principal's overseas sales manager and the dealer's sales team, the prestige which your products might bring to the dealer's company or the degree to which they serve as an entrée to other business. This joker in the pack makes the job of prioritising even more difficult and is, in fact, one of the prime reasons why I advocate action, rather than study, as the starting point for your international business.

In the medical business I particularly remember New Zealand in this context. Heaven knows the initial readings weren't good. Time-consuming and costly to reach; very small population; only average priority and spending on healthcare; tottering economy strategically over-dependent on dairy and lamb – and so forth. Also, the distributor we elected to run with wasn't too smart. As an example, he had his general sales force calling on general practitioners on a cycle of eight calls per year with nothing to sell to them except medical instruments. Now even the giants in the highly profitable pharmaceutical field couldn't afford to call on general practice doctors this frequently. There was simply no way our distributor could pay for eight calls on doctors scattered all over New Zealand, selling only the occasional medical instrument worth a few hundred dollars. Of course this distributor later went into liquidation, but not before he had established our line of medical instruments as the clear market leader in New Zealand. He had also pumped New Zealand doctors up to a higher level of purchase and use of these types of instrument than doctors in most other comparable countries. Finally our position became almost inviolable because no competitor could endure the cost of displacing us and survive!

There is no library, no reference book, no trade manual, no statistical source which can predict such factors – only experience.

In Search of Fools

The fact of the matter is that very often, especially at the early stages of building up a business in a particular country, what are needed are fools, not clever people. Clever distributors often do their calculations and frequently may conclude that the investment cycle to profitability with your products is too long – that the amount of money to be spent in building up to a level of profitable sales just wouldn't be justified by the eventual return. If all the dealers in the country were clever and did this sum then one would be in a real pickle, and would be forced to spend the money oneself in an unprofitable direct launch or perhaps to back off the market altogether. There are some other compromise solutions, such as a joint venture with another company in the same boat; however, all of these have trade-offs. By far the best solution is to find a fool. A fool who doesn't do the sums and who gets you a profitable market share without weighing the cost, or, at least, weighs it too late to change direction! Again it is difficult to assess this factor, but it is important and will often account for a country with very poor theoretical readings totally out-performing another which would have been the first selection on paper. So this point will become highly relevant when interviewing prospective distributors – probing under certain circumstances to see how foolish they are! And it is also very relevant when trying to explain performance anomalies at board presentations or at the monthly management meeting.

This phenomenon is also closely related to another, which we'll deal with later when we look at the way key performers within dealer companies can make your products successful despite the combined idiocy and apathy of all the other relevant dealer staff.

Statistical Mass

Other useful sources of data are the special market surveys and industry reports published today by a wide variety of organis-ations, both private and public. The trick is to use these sources without being consumed by them – and this is not easy. Once you are 'discovered', you are going to receive at least three kilos a week of solicitations and menus of essential reading for anyone with a hint of export work in their job specification: market research tomes on anything from a needle to an anchor and a steal at $2,750 a piece (unauthorised photocopying illegal); Asia news-letters, Africa newsletters, marketing broadsheets, electronics newsletters, agribusiness letters, global economic surveys, Department of Commerce surveys, Export Board sector news-letters; Industry Association bulletins, newsletters and reports.

This kind of industry data has become big business in its own right and is now extending to the audio–visual, so that if you have any time to spare from your reading you can now attend a plethora of conferences and seminars on related topics. The trick is to use this data sparingly and cautiously as another useful factor in grading your opportunities overseas. Later on it will become more useful as a tool with which to beat and goad distributors during arguments on market share, annual goals and level of effort. Use it in the early stages of territory analysis to understand the relative economies of different countries, to understand the basis of their economies and how this will affect the type of products you will be selling, to appreciate fundamental differences in the general culture and in their technical and consumer cultures which might affect your business.

At the very least, a firm grasp of a country's general statistics, and the industry statistics which relate to your products, will help you to relax when you get down to the all-important task of talking to those who really known what's going on – a sort of face saver. Later, when you're in a stronger position, this data will always be useful in the daily hectoring and bullying involved in bending distributors to your will. The more mature you become in a market the more relevant will be the industry statistical data in checking out sales plans, targets and marketing strategies in general.

What I have said is, I suppose, somewhat critical. This is primarily because I am addressing the problem of getting a company into the export business from scratch. Remember that in this situation the all-consuming goals are representation and supply. Until these are in place you'll sell nothing. Therefore I feel it is vital to keep a somewhat jaundiced eye on these reports and statistics and to keep the time on them to a minimum. Another reason for my scepticism is the inherent unreliability of many of these reports and surveys. You can prove this to yourself any time by taking a survey on the same topic from two different sources and comparing the contents. Or take a look at a newsletter which deals with some item very familiar to you and compare their data with the facts. It's frightening.

The Horse's Mouth

Bottom line on this subject is that at these early stages, by far the best, most selective and efficient way to accumulate a relevant database is through discussion with people already experienced in your industry sector in a particular country. Commerce Department or Export Board overseas personnel are quite good, but only in the broad sense of brushing-in the industry background as it relates to a certain market. There is no question about the value of a meeting with the British Export Board industrial electronics specialist in Hong Kong before moving on that market, and Mainland China, with a holographic printer. He'll very quickly appraise you of the idiosyncracies of doing business in Hong Kong and China in general, and more specifically in relation to your product sector. He'll teach you about capillary distribution in tiny Hong Kong but centralised purchasing in China. You'll learn from him that you will need a Hong Kong based representative, or distributor, to tackle the Chinese market – one who has the contacts and influence with the Republic's bureaucracy and decision-makers which are vital for business. He'll tell you of the push–pull situation in regard to availability of foreign funds, in China, for imports. And he can certainly help identify whether your products are currently favoured for importation, whether or not they come under national security export restrictions, and what, if any, safety standards apply to your equipment in Hong Kong and in China.

Of even greater value, however, will be a discussion with someone who is already involved through Hong Kong, in some sort of related business. This point cannot be over-emphasised. At the cost of an air fare and a hotel bill you can tap processed, graded, filtered data from someone who has been on the cutting edge of commercial reality. He can tell you how long it is taking to get payment on Chinese letters of credit, which Chinese trade shows are effective, the facts on distributor inventory policies in Hong Kong, specially relevant contract clauses with wily Hong Kong dealers. Most important of all, he can give you an infinitely more accurate indication of market potential and a factual interpretation of what all those general statistics mean in terms of business for your company. He, more than anyone else, can help you decide whether you should put Hong Kong before Taiwan, Korea, Singapore or Australia in the batting order which you will need to establish to grow your business effectively.

Choose Your Mount

A word of warning. Such helpful people are hard to find. There will usually be a natural reticence over passing on data to you free of charge which may have cost them a small fortune and a lot of time to accumulate. Alternatively, if the source is smart he may perceive a threat in parting with this data. Remember that even though you are not a direct competitor you might end up using some of his existing distributors and prove an unwelcome diversion to his distributors' sales staff. And if he is foolish enough to pass on good data without a thought, then the information which he gives should be suspect and treated with caution. He may try to use you for some obscure purpose such as guiding you to a particular distributor to gain credit with that company or, worse, for some sort of disinformation strategy which he might need at that time to steer his dealer in some Confucian direction.

The secret is to find some way to motivate the selected individual to part with the facts. Look therefore for naïvety but not stupidity. With no intention to offend, you might choose your target on ethnic grounds – for instance, choosing an American before choosing an Italian, French or Chinese source. Americans, at best, tend to part freely with good data on the basis of 'what's good for the industry is good for us' – at worst, because they tend to be more naïve in international horse-trading than the more experienced and ancient traders from Europe and Asia. This is very understandable in view of the historic weight of the internal US economy.

Another ploy is to look for a source with a big ego – although this carries the inherent risk that although he may sing like a canary to impress you with his grasp of the market, his ego may have prevented him from grasping it at all. There is one effective way to take normally non-egotistical people and force them to protect their images – by using industry associations. Here, say in the Holographic Identification Association, you can put knowledgeable sources in front of a microphone and force them to part with reasonable market intelligence to protect their egos! Or draw them into discussion groups where they will choose not to misinform for fear of discovery by their peers.

There is always the oysters and beer routine, though this type of purposeful entertainment will rarely be successful with senior staff and is therefore rarely highly valuable. Wining and dining probably works best with junior executives. Underlings in distribution companies invest enormous amounts of time dreaming of ways to get into business for themselves, and are usually willing to trade a lot of valuable market data in return for a chance to impress you and maybe get a crack at acquiring an agency. Alternatively and equally, they will want to make an impression on you so that they might be considered for any plum jobs stemming from your intended operations. You will be amazed at the sensitive and valuable data which can be easily elicited using copious beer or good wine as a catalyst. It is a well-known fact that some companies go to the lengths of advertising for personnel for fictitious jobs for just this kind of research.

The objective, anyway, at the end of this research phase, is that you will end up with a list of those countries that appear to represent good opportunities for your products and that you will be able, based again on your research, to grade these on a priority basis. You will have developed a broad picture, for each of these prioritised countries, of which of your products will be relevant and of any really serious regulatory issues. Even more important, for each of the targeted countries you will have developed preliminary, even crude contacts with potential customers and distributors. These will form the all-important seed contacts which you will later use to form an idea of the distribution mechanisms which you will need and which will provide valuable introductions to companies and people who might fit your model. Hopefully all of this will have been accomplished relatively quickly, with a sense of urgency, stemming from your conviction that the faster you arrange representation and supply, even of a compromise nature, the faster you'll find out what is really going on in a country and the faster you'll get the all-important orders!

3

MECHANISMS

We have heavily emphasised speed and pragmatism during the research and analysis period. However, as one approaches the selection and contracting phases a more sober pace is called for. A stitch in time here will save thousands later.

Horses for Courses

The first task here is to choose, for a particular country, that distribution mechanism which will bring the best overall results. By definition the way in which products will be represented and sold will vary from country to country. This fact cannot be all that obvious, if one is to judge from the large number of companies who think and talk in terms of a semi-standard approach to moving product in countries which are far from being either standard or even remotely similar in their ways of doing business. There is often a blinkered adherence to a well-proven domestic formula for distribution. This happens most often, of course, with companies based in large and more insular domestic economies. The more successful they are domestically, the more arrogant they may become in trying to fit a square plug into a round hole. It seems strange, in this day and age of jet travel, satellite broadcasting, facsimile and database, that one would have to labour the enormous differences in varying national markets. Yet any experienced export sales manager will confirm the inordinate amount of time that has to be spent, on an ongoing basis, preventing home office personnel reverting to the simplistic. Unfortunately, also, the system always defaults to error. In a situation of confusion, stress or just lack of energy the assumption will be that things are the same as, not different from, those which are familiar on the home market. Even the simplest and most obvious differences have to be taught, over and over – customs procedures, import clearance delays, currency exchange restrictions, import permits, duties, service regulations, product registration formalities, tender regulations, price controls, financial reporting requirements and so forth. The lessons are never fully learned. Generations later, export clerks, confronted with a request for a pro-forma invoice, will still mutter: 'The ass has a price list, why can't he just send a cheque with his purchase order?'

When there are palpable differences between countries such as language, culture, economy, currencies – what reason do we have to suspect that their ways of doing business will be the same? In fact they are not, and a mature international distribution network will reflect the difference in trading practices from country to country.

Some Classics

SOLE: A relatively small country such as Denmark suggests a single national distributor. Exclusivity will probably be needed to keep the sales volumes at an interesting level for the distributor and so retain his enthusiasm. Shared distribution would represent an uninteresting slice of a small pie.

EXCLUSIVE: Fundamentals of the Japanese national and business culture heavily favour a national exclusive dealership, and the opportunities of scale and market size are usually best tackled using a sub-distribution network supplied and serviced by the national exclusive importer. The extra cost layers create interesting pricing challenges and there will be an enormous strategic dependence on the exclusive importer. However, of all the world markets, Japan is the one where a very highly motivated dealer is essential in tackling the unique regulatory and trading idiosyncrasies which are a feature of Japan's commercial life.

MULTIPLE: Conversely, a much larger territory such as the United Kingdom, depending on volumes and profitability, might accommodate multiple independent distribution without serious loss of motivation. This can provide tremendous opportunities to share the franchise out between specialist distributors who individually concentrate on specific market sectors. If, for example, you were selling a mechanical paint-stripper, you might select one distributor who has focus and established outlets to the domestic household market, and another altogether independent dealer whose sales force concentrates exclusively on industrial outlets. Or you might choose one company for the south of England and Wales which concentrates on both domestic and industrial markets, but other separate distributors for the North of England, Scotland and Northern Ireland. Each would, in theory, have enough sales volume and profits to justify a vigorous sales programme, and also to allow them to turn a blind eye to the inevitable territorial infringements and irritations that accompany a split franchise.

TIED: In a considerable number of situations the prestige of direct importation is a major incentive. In these cases a principal national distributor can be persuaded to allow other smaller regional companies to import the product directly from the factory to allow the essential saving of face. Compensation for his investments in national promotion of the product, national advertising, trade shows and such will be by way of commission payment to him on all direct shipments to these smaller regional dealers – this commission may or may not be visible to the regional importers, depending on the situation.

TERRITORIAL: Switzerland would seem to call for a national exclusive but is frequently better served by independent dealers who follow that country's ethnic divisions and are specialised in selling to its four communities.

NON-STOCKING: For many of the closed economies, particularly in the Eastern bloc, stocking distributors will be out of the question. Neither currency nor import permits will be available. In many cases, all purchasing of the type of commodity in question will be conducted through central government purchasing offices by some sort of tendering procedure. In such cases an agent or manufacturer's representative will be the norm, funded by commissions paid on successful bids. Furthermore, successful agents are often best located outside the bloc, operating through recognised access points in Berlin, Vienna, Venice, Helsinki and the like.

Again, really small economies like Guam, Sri Lanka, Burma, Fiji, South Yemen and so on just cannot justify carrying inventory for the level of available business. Other countries, while big in size and population, just don't have the funds to hold inventory. Here profits and cash-flow in representation companies will be so low that even importation costs would pose an unbearable strain. So most countries in these types of situation can only be serviced by a commission agent. In some cases even these are not viable, and purchasing will be done direct by governments through an overseas government purchasing mission or through designated overseas purchasing consultants.

SUBSIDIARIES AND PARTNERS: Other situations can be vastly more complex. In Germany, for example, distribution of popular types of product tends to be highly capillary. Population and regional economies are quite homogeneously dispersed, and each significant population centre, and they are myriad, is well serviced through locally based and stocked representation. Consequently it is often difficult to find an effective truly national distributor. Local competition is too proliferous and too close to the market, yet thrives due to the extraordinary buoyancy and size of the consumer base.

Sometimes penetration by local suppliers is so efficient that even regional distributors are not viable. All of this, of course, applies only to product with a wide and dispersed customer base. Obviously it would not apply, say, to automotive component manufacturers which could be very well served by a national house. However, it would almost certainly apply to the distribution of hand tools, for which every city and town in Germany would have its bevy of wholesalers. In such situations an exporter can be faced with very high entry costs and risks. A preliminary attempt to reach the huge number of local distributors through a national importer will probably fail, since such houses will not provide the level of customer service demanded by the stringent German trading ethic. Sometimes the only solution, and one which carries a high cost, is to establish a direct importation and distribution subsidiary, thus adequately controlling issues of service, price, delivery and so forth.

There are countries where the forces in favour of the purchase of domestic made product are exceptionally and prohibitively strong. A classic example would be France, where a mixture of genuine natural chauvinism and legendary government creativity in frustrating imports especially militates against technically less sophisticated consumables. In such situations one would tend to look beyond simple distribution solutions and seriously weigh mechanisms such as joint ventures with established French companies, attaching a nationally recognised brand name to the product, licensing manufacture to a domestic producer, or investing directly, through branch or subsidiary, in a national French identity.

The fact is that the options to be considered for distribution are practically infinitely variable and cannot easily be defined or listed. They are like rivers – some straight, uniformly deep and wide, others complex with tributaries and deltas, rapids and falls. Developing and refining distribution channels is a life's study with little substitute for experience.

Broad Options

The important thing, during the early stages of building up a distribution network, is to think flexibly and to realise that what is sauce for the goose will not necessarily please the gander. You should also realise that due to limited resources – you may well be the only export executive in the company – some compromises will have to be made initially for the sake of getting the ball rolling. The prime mechanisms to consider are: sole national fully exclusive; multiple national but exclusive by product sector; regional national exclusive by geographical area; national exclusive with regional sub-dealer; and finally, simple commission-agent representative.

Since even these more limited selections still consume a lot of time, you may want to consider a further shortening of the options: sole national fully exclusive; multiple national but exclusive by product sector. You will find that sub-dealers will develop in any event as a natural progression of a tied national exclusivity. Commission agents will often be naturally dictated by the circumstances and usually associated with a somewhat lower priority.

Remember, however, that change and the gradual sophistication of your distribution channels are inevitable and that this must be planned for, especially when finding and contracting with distributors. Agreements with new-found business partners must allow for change and protect you during the process of maturing your channels.

The Rule

There is a sacred tenet, a fundamental immutable rule in the selection of both the mechanisms themselves and the companies you will choose to fit those mechanisms: you must, first and foremost, talk to the final customers, those who will ultimately buy and use your product – or one similar.

Lies and Evasions

From Chapter 1 you will remember that distributors, like horse-traders, have a divine right to lie and cheat in order to protect a franchise. Well, naturally, they will assume the same right when it comes to securing any franchise which they would consider valuable to their business.

Confronted with the possibility of securing a distribution franchise for a potentially profitable product line, a distributor's primary goal is to get the offer of the franchise. Even when time is short the strategy is always the same – fail safe – get the offer first! There will be plenty of time later to decide whether or not profits will be adequate, whether or not the product dovetails with existing lines – or even if the product is saleable in the country! The point is that such study and decision process runs the risk of being a frustrating waste of time unless the offer of distribution rights is assured. Skilled distributors will therefore simply probe to establish what you see as the requirements of an adequate distributor – your ground rules for selection for the dealership. They will then present only those facts, and draw only on that evidence which supports their application and claims.

If you are looking for a large sales force they will hire people from the streets to fill their sales conference room for your presentation. They will draft in cleaning ladies and clerks as sales personnel for a day. They will conjure up fabulous maps, with a plethora of pins and tapes to establish the illusion of territorial coverage. Warehouse staff become commercial managers for a day, and ageing sales staff dust off old marketing tomes and rehearse the vocabulary of Marketing Mix, Gaussian Distributions and Vertical Markets.

Inevitably new corporate structures are fantasised and betrayed on glossy new paper by their fresh ink. A thousand slide photographs of the same modest office and warehouse are flashed rapidly and non-sequentially to create the illusion of corporate strength and resource. Sales staff already overworked with excess product lines will be touted as special product managers who will devote their efforts to the management of your line. And of course the number of other lines held will be underplayed in the first place, with only the prestige lines being mentioned as a further seduction. Of course, any lines that could be considered even remotely competitive to the one you are offering are dethroned for the day and exiled out of sight! Showrooms, offices and, of course, warehouses will be purged of anything likely to interfere with the negotiation.

Needless to say, if the prospective company's big size is seen as a threat, divisionalisation will be invoked and focus and specialisation will be emphasised. If the company's small size is perceived as a hazard, revenues will be grossly exaggerated or, at the very least, historical figures will be ignored and only current 'targets' discussed. A vocabulary of evasion will permeate every discussion and correspondence. You will hear of branch 'facilities' in the South and additional selling 'personnel' in the North. Money, and the capacity to invest in inventory, will be 'no problem' – neither, of course, will it be quantified!

We will see later how to screen and check all the nonsense thrown at prospective principals in these situations, but the most effective protection of all is a pre-screening, with end-users, prior to any intercourse whatsoever with dealers.

Define the Customers

Before you set about learning from customers, however, you have to define clearly who your customers will be. Naturally you will include those who will end up using your product. However, these people – end-users – may not be the first people either to specify, or to buy, your product. There may, for instance, be consultants or system designers in the loop between you and the end-user. Alternatively your product may be purchased by another manufacturer to use as a component in equipment which he later sells to the end-user. And, of course, the most common intermediate purchasers between you and the end-user are so-called retailers. Sometimes these retailers may form a part of your selected distributor organisation – but if not, then they also have to be looked upon as customers.

So, define your customers clearly and then make arrangements to learn from them before even thinking of choosing a distribution channel or talking to any prospective dealers.

What, Why, How, When and Where?

Try to learn from these all-important customers what they buy, why they buy it, how they buy it, when they buy it and where they buy it.

WHAT? It's fair to assume that during the analysis phase you've done the basic research on competitive product in a market and so will know roughly how your product stacks against the competition. Now you take the chance to put a batting order on the customer's preferences for both manufacturer and product features. You'll be able to tease out gaps in your product line, anomalies in pricing, specification changes and performance issues way before any prospective dealer gets to know of them. Some of the feature preferences can possibly be addressed before going to market. At the very least, however, you will be able to go into distributor negotiations with a clear idea of where the product problems will lie. And you will be able to prepare counter-arguments, in advance, for those aspects of your product performance, or price, that are problematic. And, of course, with a clearer first-hand idea of what the customer wants, you will be able to counter a lot of false negatives and rubbish from prospective dealers – who save and hoard negatives as valuable defence weapons for later skirmishes.

WHY? Essentially this is establishing the stimulus for purchase. Is it impulse-based on advertising or mail-shot? Does it come from editorials in trade journals? Does the sale usually result from a sales call and product demonstration? Is it stimulated by an annual budgeted contract for supplies purchase? What part do trade shows or exhibitions play?

HOW? This is really a study of the steps involved from the moment interest is generated in a product to the point where an actual physical purchase order is generated. Great care must be taken to identify the decision-makers and to distinguish them from those who actually support, or promote, the purchase but don't have the power to generate an order. Of course, selling has to be done to both of these groups and they are mutually inter-dependent. The simplest purchase will be an impulse-buy from a consumer in a retail store. At the other end of the scale of complexity will be the purchase of military supplies or power-generating equipment, which will invariably involve complex and highly political purchasing committees in addition to hosts of technical, financial, service and purchasing functionaries.

WHEN? There may be significant seasonal variations in sales level, the obvious examples being ski equipment, heating appliances or educational devices. Other variations may be more subtle and may be tied to issues such as local tax situations, where professionals, for example, may find it tax-effective to load some capital purchases into the last hours of the financial tax year. Again, purchasing budgets for government departments and services, military organisations, healthcare departments and so forth are usually expended during predictable periods, and sales efforts outside of these periods can be a waste of time. At the risk of stating the obvious, it will be well nigh impossible to sell anything in the Arab countries during the feast of Ramadan in the early part of the year, and business is, to put it mildly, sluggish in the entire southern half of Europe during July and August. And so on.

Here also we would cover the question of required delivery times. This is both a vital and a tricky issue. Vital, in that it is the key to your competitiveness – tricky in that it will define the level of inventory in which your distributors will need to invest to be competitive. This in turn will have big implications for pricing and credit terms.

WHERE? The thumbnail sketch of your potential customers and their purchasing idiosyncrasies is filling out nicely. Where they purchase will really begin to define the structure you will choose to supply them. Do they look for competitive price quotations from different suppliers? Or do they tend to purchase loyally from a company with a good service reputation? Will they scout nationally for the product or will they favour purchase from local dealers? Again, do they usually shop at a well-known, widely-stocked distributor in one of the bigger cities, or do they go to smaller but more specialised dealers?

The reasons for the customer's choice of supplier will be tied closely to the previous questions of what he prefers, and why, how and when he buys.

Who?

The final part of this whole process of interview with the potential customer group is the vital part of customer reference. Put simply, this is getting the names from the customer of the companies who supply him, the reasons why he chooses them, the names of salesmen who call on him regularly. In effect, a sort of poll of the customer to establish who does a good job, in his area, of product representation and who does not. It is the perfect time to check out those companies which have already approached you or which you have already dredged up from exhibitions, trade shows, journals, trade societies and the study of parallel distributors! If it is done correctly you can emerge from a series of customer interviews with a beautifully graded list of who does a good job in a particular area and who does not.

Don't Be Put Off

So, talking to the customer is the starting point for choosing the distribution mechanism that you are going to use, and also provides a qualified listing of companies who are perceived to do the job well. These, to say the least, are valuable achievements – so don't be easily deterred from this exercise. Prioritise it. Insist on it. The dark forces will be against you. Time and pressure for early results will tempt you to take a short cut and to take, at face value, the assertions of a dealer bidding for your business. Giving in to these pressures is really tantamount to Russian roulette – sometimes you win, sometimes you lose. It is nothing more than a game of chance. It is not, in golfing parlance, the percentage play.

Language can be a much bigger problem when working with end-users – as opposed to distributors, who normally have language capabilities as a tool. But don't let language stand in the way. Hire an interpreter, travel with a consultant, but for heaven's sake don't skip this vital stage. It can also be done quickly. You don't have to go for a textbook statistical sample – a few quick calls to appropriate people in the major population centres, a few extra days per country, and enough will be achieved.

Sometimes it can actually be short-circuited, or numerically enhanced, by going to good end-user exhibitions or congresses and conducting the interviews there. The results can also be improved by direct contact with trade or professional associations, where a good discussion with the secretariat, over some oysters, can elicit the distilled wisdom of the group!

Don't be put off by the apparent success of others who have omitted this step – what they don't realise, and certainly will never share, is the time lost in throwing a blind dart. The really comfortable fact is that you will be in the driving seat from the beginning, selecting how you want to channel your merchandise and selecting those whom you want to consider as components in that structure – and playing with a much stronger deck of cards in all the ensuing haggling and dealing!

4

SELECTION

By this stage, hopefully, we have succeeded in changing some attitudes and preconceptions on how to get going in international selling. While a lot of what we've said may be old hat to more seasoned hands, the fact remains that I haven't seen one novice go about his export start-up correctly for quite some years. On the contrary, I see them routinely and almost ritually walking into the same old traps: going directly to trade shows and negotiating immediately with distribution companies without completing any independent work in the actual marketplace; studiously noting and accepting at face value all sorts of unqualified data and statistics; junketing with trade missions and conducting endless fatuous interviews with the kind of opportunists these road shows attract – and other dreadful displays of naïvety, ignorance and indiscretion.

Vultures

These poor apprentices represent a succulent catch for the buzzards of the distribution business, the line-gatherers – those individuals who travel the international circuit, year in year out, looking for virgin franchises to prop up their failing businesses. They come, of course, well tooled with corporate brochures, organisational charts, reams of market statistics and mounted tracts on corporate philosophy, mission and strategy. It's fun

spotting them and tracking their movements from year to year
and there's no better way of relieving a dull moment at a flagging
exhibition than to watch them work over fresh prey. Usually
their companies are dead from the neck up – leaderless small
outfits overloaded with mismatching lines, insensible to any
market guidance or any real sales planning. They will long since
have abandoned any real pretension to securing a market or
being truly competitive. Rather they have learned to live in an
interminable wake, where they sustain themselves by gathering
new product lines as fast as older ones are taken from them.
These new lines do provide some sales, however minimal, and
some cash-flow, if not profit. Margins for the first few months
will be enormous, since they will have culled the product from
their newest victim at 'sampling' prices – if not entirely free.
Additionally, they will probably succeed in bullying unpro-
tected credit for their first shipments, which will be a further
source of profit in the likely event that the new relationship will
rupture savagely within a few months.

The vultures are usually accompanied by a bag-carrier cum
drinking companion whose official title will change from day to
day to suit the needs of the occasion. He is easily identified by his
fetid breath, bloodshot eyes and general disembodiment from
events around him. His main function, apart from porterage,
drinking and procurement, is to support his master's invective
with his body language during meetings. His clothing will
usually be well stained with beer, and often a condom or two will
fall out of his wallet if, and when, he offers a business card.

Initial approaches vary. Some try to come in hard, sweeping
onto the stage with: 'Quickly, is there someone with authority
here? I leave for London in less than an hour! I need your
immediate best export distributor prices for shower heads in
quantities of 5,000 up to 100,000, delivered New Delhi within
six weeks!' Of course all but the experienced will fall into
immediate submission and the stage will be set for one concession after another to retain his 'interest'. Appointments will
be made for visits to New Delhi to discuss 'finalisation of the
business relationship' – exclusive, naturally. Best net prices will
be readily surrendered. Impressive bank references will be
exchanged and letters of credit and other forms of credit protection discussed openly and, seemingly, with confidence. Then the

inevitable afterthought as they dash to the London flight: 'By the way, dear Norman, we will need the samples within two weeks if the deal is to be closed – so send 100 each of the chrome, natural copper and brass plated. Have your staff telex air waybill number and flight numbers to Devender here. We will need to act quickly to have them cleared in time for the demonstrations . . .'

'Er, Mr Dandekar, er . . . we don't have a free sample policy . . . I, er . . . I could give a special discount . . . I . . .'

'Oh! Really? What is this special discount?'

'Er . . . net less twenty five per cent . . .'

'Really? Oh well, ship them anyway. But we will need to discuss market support when you get to New Delhi!'

'Yes, sure . . . er . . . how about payment . . .?'

'No problem. We will pay you cash for these and we can discuss credit terms in New Delhi. I must leave – we'll miss the flight!'

'OK, OK. Er . . . when will you pay the cash?'

'Straight away, when we get the documents. Goodbye. We really must go, dear Norman. Bye-bye!'

Others will take an indirect sales approach. Their materials will heavily emphasise their contacts. Their companion may, instead, be a member of a royal family or a retired senior officer in the military. Nothing overt will be said. There will be plenty of Rolex and gold amulet flashed. They will merely want to 'study' the possibilities with your product. If you show signs of being particularly vulnerable there may even be threats, talks of black-lists, approvals procedures, advisory bodies and so forth. Various enormous current tenders will be bandied, and potential sales in telephone numbers. Of course, there will be no purpose for a further meeting, or a visit, until they have evaluated your product and its potential. Samples . . .

Many have learned to role-play like chameleons and are, in their own right, gifted actors. They are quick to establish your expectations with skilled probing during the initial foreplay. Like a good salesman they will listen for a while, teasing out your background, likes and dislikes, and then tailoring their pitch to suit. For an American supplier their eyes will light up with aggressiveness and they will talk of 'getting out there and selling the product in, beating the bushes . . .' If it is a Japanese supplier the emphasis will naturally be on team, consensus, careful prestudy, meticulous service arrangements, and so forth. To an Italian they will underline key contacts and a policy of placing enormous initial stocking orders – after the sampling, of course! For younger Scandinavian executives they are not above touting beautiful female marketing assistants and insisting on visits to their country for situation 'studies'.

Bullying can assume all sorts of guises. A favourite is where, sensing a lack of commitment, a dealer may hint, albeit apologetically, that without your product – which he accepts as the best – he may be forced to saturate the market with an inferior but highly profitable model, made in Eastern Europe. Of course, he would be reluctant to do such a thing – but, naturally, he can't stand by and let the business go to a competitor!

I have faced people who have been on the verge of physical violence. I remember a meeting in Utrecht where an enormous bearded Dutchman shrieked that he would ruin us in Belgium if we didn't give the line to an affiliate. He produced extensive advertising and brochure artwork, featuring our products, as evidence to his intention to buy our merchandise elsewhere and dump in Belgium. This would demotivate our current dealer, devalue the franchise and presumably consign us to the Dutchman's care for ever afterwards! Each threat was reinforced with a fist on the table. Actually, he carried out his threat, but we had a trick or two ourselves.

Vulnerability

These and many more different types of approach are fairly easy to recognise and resist when one has experience under the belt and also, perhaps, a well-established and growing business. They can be much harder to counter, however, with inexperience, with pressure to get orders and, especially, when one hasn't done the groundwork to counter the lies and exaggerations. And there is always the fear of rejecting what might have amounted to a really good business opportunity.

Sometimes, also, there are countries which are relatively low on your priority list and where pre-screening, let alone a visit, has had to be deferred for a considerable time. On the basis that any distributor is better than none, one sometimes has to take a flyer and part with the agency on the offchance of getting some opportunity business. This is fine, and we will see that many of our dealer screening measures can still be applied. As a practical measure to stack the odds, however, look for these points: look for someone who has studied your product before his meeting; look for a dealer who comes prepared with some hard data on his territory as it applies to your product; look for a candidate who comes with specific information on your competitors. All these items point to a serious interest in exploiting your product and to at least some vestiges of professionalism. In addition to our other screening tests, offer absolutely no concessions on sample prices and insist on fully protected payment until a track record is established. If these later items are fairly readily accepted then there is a fighting chance that you've found a serious distributor. Finally, on this subject, make sure that the franchise is offered on a trial basis only and for no more than six months to a year. The statistical probability is that it won't work out!

Following suggestions so far will result in a pretty clear idea of how to go about selling product in priority countries and will have generated a list of those that need screening as potential cogs in a distribution wheel. It should hardly be necessary to state that data which you will start to accumulate, as you interview and profile distributors, should be recorded in some fairly uniform way. It would be an insult to specify the format and a host of silly details. Suffice it to say that these records build up into a very useful data bank for future reference as requirements change.

Checks and Balances

There is a trick to the method and sequence of recording dealer data. On your first meeting with a prospect you should adopt a seemingly casual attitude towards records. In fact, you should appear to take none. Put away the notebook and focus on the dealer, consigning the data, for the moment, to memory. This could happen, for instance, in the morning during an exhibition – or in the early and preliminary discussions at his offices, say before lunch. At the first opportunity, privately jot down the key data – claimed turnover, number of sales staff, number of branches, number of service technicians and so forth. Later on, during more detailed meetings, or during a wrap-up session, take out a pad and ask once again for the same basic statistics. Privately again, compare the two sets of data. It is incredible how rarely they match. It is a characteristic of habitual liars that they get careless and over-confident. Keep the inconsistencies to yourself, however, and don't show your hand or a red alert will go out and further checks will be much more difficult.

Other questions can be used as mathematical cross-checks on the dealer's claims. In the morning, focus only on his sales volumes. In the afternoon, talk about his inventory level and, innocuously, about how often he manages to turn his inventory. Sadly, again, the two sets of data will rarely correlate to the same sales figures. One would imagine that even the dullest would see that their sales claims for individual product lines at least approximated to the stated company total. Again there will be wide disparity, which cannot be accounted for by contributions from the minor lines. These cross checks are useful, not necessarily for detecting liars – for most are – but for refining the data, approximating reality and defining the enemy!

The other great area of conjure relates to staff, both in numbers and in function. Confrontational checks here really don't work very well, because they will usually be prepared for cross-examination and be ready to go to ground on the basis of language, confusionism or an urgent appointment. The best technique is to lull first and then bluff. If you suspect the Karachi salesman of being, in reality, the janitor, take him to one side and say that you hope he found the day interesting and that you would love to see him take up sales full-time, that he has a natural ability for selling! It's like baiting fish, and quite exciting when you make a catch – his eyes glow with zeal and he whispers confidentially to you that this is his dream! Take the fellow who has been touted as a specialist product manager in your product area and quietly congratulate him on his new appointment. If that's his role for the day he really has no option but to accept graciously. If he has genuinely been doing the job for some time he'll quickly want to let you know.

The salesmen, of course, also provide excellent opportunities to check data on sales volumes provided by management –

especially at unguarded moments or over cocktails. In fact, practically everyone in the building can be used to qualify data – secretaries, accounting clerks (who find it more difficult to lie than most), service personnel and, of course, the receptionist. Needless to say, you will not get very far if your questions are seen to be purposeful. They have to be subtle, indirect and casual – and the results can be astounding. You might find out, for example, that most of the staff work for another company, that the premises are not exclusive to your dealer and that several of the Cebu salespeople actually live in Metro Manila.

On one of the best grazings I've had, some years ago in Nice, I discovered that the managing director was sleeping with the credit controller, the marketing manager was sleeping with the managing director's wife, my salesman was sleeping with the receptionist and the financial controller was a practising homosexual and a thief! You may ask of what value was all this data? I can say, at least, that it gave me a certain insight into the company's focus!

Simulation and dissimulation are the everyday tools of companies trying to attract agencies. Some efforts at deception are obviously outrageous, but some are quite subtle and often carry the approval of the commercial community at large. Take a certain distributor we looked at closely once in Brisbane as a potential national house for electrical switchgear. On preliminary interview the company's strengths seemed formidable. The suburban premises were very large and impressively populated. Entrance and foyer were striking, with a substantial array of brass number plates announcing one subsidiary after another. During the normal profiling questions about the organisation the answers were strangely non-evasive and very impressive: twenty field sales staff, branch offices in all other states; service/repair facilities, staffed by qualified engineers in Sydney, Melbourne, Adelaide and Perth; and a bevy of specialised senior staff in market development, advertising, promotion and so forth. In fact, a relatively new salesman for our company decided to look no further and committed the franchise for twelve months.

The first telltale sign was an inconsistent reluctance to place any meaningful stocking orders and further sinister complications when it came to paying even for the modest ones placed. Nor were the agreed sales and promotional activities materialising. I had to take a fast trip out to Brisbane to try to unravel the mystery. On arrival, the factor which puzzled me most was the penchant for very complex corporate structures and subsidiaries. From my experiences elsewhere, particularly working for individualists and entrepreneurs during my earlier career, I had come to associate an unhealthy and unbalanced focus on corporate structures with weak underlying finances. So we focused our probing on the corporate structure and fairly quickly established that we were, in fact, trading with a company with only eight employees, of whom two were in sales and the rest were secretarial or administrative. In reality we were in the midst of a honeycomb of similar small companies in maintenance, advertising, public relations and computer peripheral sales. Each had a nominal shareholding in an umbrella company from which they drew their names as subsidiaries. The individual companies within the hive did, in fact, co-operate with each other periodically. But the main co-operation was in assisting each other in duping the unwary with fictitious staff and financial resources. I believe the scheme won an industry award in Australia. I suppose the award itself was concocted by the public relations cellmate!

Verification

By grasping the fundamentals, conducting a sensible efficient analysis and choosing good structures by talking to customers, we have set ourselves in a very powerful position for making selections. In effect we're going into the arena feeling fit and with a clear gameplan. We have a very well-defined shopping list and we are not going to be distracted by other items on the shelf – no matter how brightly they are packed. When interviewing a distributor we know clearly where he would fit in our grand scheme of things and we know what he will need to get the job done for us. So the interviewing process is simply making sure we cover all the bases in terms of things we need to know, and thereafter a vital and enjoyable process of verification. Much of this verification can be done on the spot during interview.

This interview is far better conducted at the distributor's premises because of the abundant opportunities for cross-check already discussed. On his premises, however, you're essentially taking on a grand master on his own ground and, no matter how adept you become at the game of checks and balances, you can't expect to leave with a full deck of cards. The final and ultimate verification must be done in the field and through independent reference. This means talking to some of the distributor's customers directly and independently, visiting some of his regional sub-distributors and, vitally, talking to some of his other main suppliers. Remember, however, to treat the information you get from other suppliers with great caution. Often they will inflate a dealer's performance just to get brownie points or to repay an old favour. Conversely they may, if they are smart, downplay a dealer's performance or completely misrepresent his strengths, hoping to deflect another franchise which would compete for their dealer's attentions! Neither can the dealer's customers be counted on for sound comment, since they too will often have old scores to settle. Probably the least reliable sources will be sub-dealers, since they will have an umbilical relationship to the distributor which they won't want to jeopardise. But, taken together, all these independent sources can provide the indispensable check on the prospective dealer's selling strengths, number of sales staff, regional coverage, other lines held, financial status, payment history and so forth.

Buy Now, Pay Later

In the business of sales our life bread, the fundamental substance from which we draw our energy and around which our commercial lives revolve, the blood without which, like Dracula, we would wither and die – is the purchase order. Any distributor worth his salt, sensing a problem with his distribution proposal or needing a closing mechanism to secure the line, will not hesitate to dangle whatever order is necessary to sway the issue. What may seem like prostitution is in reality a smart business decision. Who knows the profit potential of your product once it is well established? Who knows what value the franchise will accumulate in the future, to what other markets it might serve as entrée, what avenues it might open as reference? An excess of inventory for a few months would be considered a very small price to pay for the opportunity to explore all these possibilities.

What is certain is that he will never get the chance to explore any of these potentials if you leave his office and give the franchise to another company. In his eyes, therefore, the percentage play is to get the franchise first and decide on its real value later. His task and skill lies in gauging just what size of order is needed to close the deal and to end your search right there in his office. Later, at the contracting phase, he will probably try to negotiate clauses which will reduce his exposure in making this gesture – such as favourable return of merchandise clauses or special deferred payment for opening inventory orders. Quite often, after some study, he may decline the franchise altogether. In the meantime, however, he will have bought himself the opportunity, and some vital time, by seducing you with a well-pitched stocking order. All of us in the business, no matter how well seasoned we consider ourselves, are prey to this tactic. At the lowest level it may be an immature and naïve fledgeling who wants to arrive home like a hero with a fat stocking order and a filled short-term sales goal. Or a poorly motivated export salesman may want to short-circuit the selection routine and get home faster, maybe to take care of a domestic problem. Again, a remuneration scheme may have been poorly chosen and may pay bigger rewards for fast short-term orders than for well-executed long-term moves.

Even the most seasoned and professional have great difficulty in turning away from a whopping great stocking order enhanced considerably with features such as good lead time, single shipment and fully protected payment. It is not difficult to find ways of excusing ourselves. We know, for example, that a hefty dealer inventory is one way of ensuring that the product gets its fair share of distributor attention. It seems to take care of questions relating to a prospective dealer's aggressiveness, commitment and financial strength. And it certainly won't damage the quarterly sales report! We will comfort ourselves with the thought, which is quite true, that we never will find the perfect fit and that a bird in the hand is worth two in the bush. Finally, a good stocking order is also a criterion of a good dealership arrangement – so it is easy to become confused. But falling for the bait of a mammoth stocking order can be lethal.

Some Wrong Reasons

A distributor's reasons for going after a certain franchise are not always obvious or even logical. In the best cases a distributor will seek a new line because he knows that he can offer a supplier a reasonable market share while generating acceptable profits for himself with a line which matches his business direction and skills. On the other hand, we have already discussed some cases where lines are sought willy-nilly to prop up ailing companies and with no chance of profitable partnership. Others just are not smart enough, or professional enough, to make a good judgement. Yet again, others go after lines for very devious reasons. There is no better way to kill a potential or existing competitor than to bottle the threatening line up in a useless, inactive distribution agreement. This is often done through a sister or daughter company. The fact that a related company is dealing with one of your competitors can often be concealed or overlooked. Even if it is discovered prior to contract, there are many ways of promoting it as an advantage rather than a handicap. The real goal, however, will be absolute control of a competitor.

Another pitfall is where a distributor needs your line as a door opener for those other products on which he will really focus. Your name and reputation for quality may offer him prestige and, by implication, upgrade the perception of other lower level products in his catalogue.

He may need your products only as a filler for government bids and tenders in general. In many countries, in order to be considered for such government bids, or other volume contracts, the bidding company must quote for all items listed in the tender. A good way of having access to items not normally handled by the bidder, and at more attractive prices, is to become an authorised distributor. Once a manufacturer becomes established on the international market, and as a result starts to be specified on such tenders, he can expect to be inundated daily with solicitations for the franchise from these bidding companies. In addition to the scores which exist in each individual country, there are legions of offshore import/export companies based in opportunist locations in Miami, New York, Frankfurt, Berlin, Vienna, London, Hong Kong, Singapore and so on. Occasionally they win tenders, so the trick is to deal with them without being consumed by paperwork, without surrendering significant distribution rights and above all without ever deluding oneself into thinking that these people act as distributors!

Yet another reason why a dealer may appear to go after your line is that in reality he is going after another. He may need your line as a prestige reference or simply to provide his company with breadth which may be important in securing another franchise. Your line might begin and end as a cosmetic on a bank presentation. It might be used to substantiate false descriptions or declarations on importation documents so as to get around duties or import restrictions. We once fell for the stocking order routine in the Philippines and ended up as cover for a substantial business in the importation of Italian video pornography. The Philippines hasn't been a totally safe place now for some years and executives do have to be careful, but the first real suspicion our salesman had that things were not quite normal was when our agent kept his hand on a pistol even during lunch!

Getting the Fingers Burned

Falling for the stocking order and giving the franchise, either to a bad company or a bandit, can be an expensive error. We have talked pretty extensively about the positive reasons for choosing intelligently – but some of the negatives in making an error are just as compelling.

In a number of countries the time and cost involved in terminating a contract can be extensive, particularly in the litigious societies such as Germany, Italy and the US, where smart lawyers can procrastinate painfully and expensively. There is also the cost in lost active distribution time, the loss in business.

There is the question of dealing with national inventory of your product. Rarely is it satisfactorily transferred from an old dealer to a new one. Costly returns of goods to your factory arise, messy refurbishments and a salesman's constant bugbear – credits! Forcing the terminated dealer to swallow the merchandise is not always a good idea. He can make life very tough, even impossible, for a new distributor, by off-loading your product at or below cost and thus strangling your new dealer's sales and reputation at birth.

Changing dealerships is often bad for the market and for the customers. It creates discontinuity and results in confusion in the customer's mind and a loss of confidence in both delivery and service. In some countries there may be huge delays in restarting distribution, since products may need to go through a very lengthy re-registration procedure by the new distributor. Taiwan and Japan are examples. Termination invariably involves a credit risk, and it takes a lot of skill and experience to avoid bad debts during and after a rupture.

It is hardly necessary to emphasise the loss in time and money in retraining of dealer representatives and general staff, corrective advertising, public relations and the general re-invention of the wheel that must take place during such changes.

So the temptation to take short cuts, to forget the checks and balances, to ignore external validation, to fall for the lure of the big stocking order, must be seen in the context of the costs of failure.

In many situations, of course, full qualification of prospective distributors is either just not possible or simply not practical in terms of cost or convenience. These things have to be judged pragmatically and sensibly. Interviewing sub-distributors in Japan will not be worthwhile, as their prime loyalty to the main distributor will transcend all other considerations, including frankness. Your priorities are unlikely to dictate time for lengthy market-based checks in Mauritius. If Andorra, Bhutan or the Solomon Islands are not on your objectives schedule for the next three years, then take the stock order and run! If validation of a distributor's claims in Lebanon or Tehran means risking a life, would it really make sense to turn down a $25,000 letter of credit?

The trick, however, is to make such concessions the exception rather than the rule and to make them with a knowing and wary eye on the costs and implications.

Appetite

The question of financial strength is worthy of special attention. The first and foremost needs in a new distributor are interest, activity, motivation, commitment. Sadly, however, these characteristics are often in inverse proportion to a company's financial strength. Even those excellent companies who succeed in retaining these attributes as they grow larger and more powerful will tend to focus their positive energy on significant contributors, usually prioritised on profit contribution. Unless your product is so innovative in terms of price or performance as to offer cosmic growth prospects, it will likely be relegated and eventually suffocated somewhere in the bowels of a big organisation. A relatively new entrant to the market, with a product which will require solid market pre-preparation, a lot of detailed presentation and field demonstration, and heavy selling on product feature and benefit, will more often than not be strangled at birth in large distribution companies, where bonus–crazy department managers chase enormous annual volume increases. Later on, when a product has assumed a significant role in the market with a proven track record in sales and profits, the motives needed to make these large companies function will be in place. A line can then really start to capitalise on all the advantages of a very strong company and distribution organisation, with all that this offers in terms of sales coverage and ability to invest heavily in promotion, advertising and so forth. Almost certainly, however, in the early days of painstakingly building a market for a product, small will be beautiful and large national sales coverage and promotional strength will be better traded for appetite; for having a distributor who needs to get out and sell your product in order to eat; for having a leaner outfit focus heavily on your product as a strategic element in their whole company future.

Many of the downsides of these smaller hungrier companies are, in any case, illusory. Two or three salespeople out selling your product in order to make ends meet are worth a dozen poorly motivated and disinterested dealer salesmen. A sub-distributor network will be more effective supplied through a small importer than through a big national house which will be seen as more of a competitor to the sub-dealer than a partner.

There are more benefits – all of them revolving on focus, motivation and access – all of them coming back to the 'dentist' analogy and to balance in the relationship.

A normal challenge in selecting a leaner company with more limited resources will be the issue of payment. In this area there is a lot of naïvety and stupidity. One hears clichés such as 'we're not in the banking business' and so on. The point is that if you're in the business of building an export business, and if you have understood the fundamentals of motive and balance – then you had better darned well get into the so-called banking business, a misnomer for the creative assistance of dealers with the financing of their growth. Ways to do this while minimising your exposure to bad debt will be discussed later. For now, however, the point is that focused and more aggressive distribution often goes hand in hand with creative management of a credit exposure, and an export sales manager had better get to grips with that fact from the outset.

Clubs

As one would expect, various distributors from different industry sectors and from different countries have frequently got together in industry associations just as national dealer organisations and national retail groupings have done. All of these associations are, at their core, self-serving and designed primarily to inform and defend their members by exchanging data and acting as industry-watchers. Occasionally they succeed in co-operating to the extent of collaboration through group purchase of certain strategic supplies. Their members discovered long ago that even a hint of collective purchasing power worked wonders when trying to swing a franchise. Germany is very strong in national retail associations – as one would expect in such a capillary retail model.

In general, groups are to be avoided. Where this is impossible, their existence should be known but factored very carefully. The possibility of wide market entry through group purchase rarely materialises, since the individual cells within the group will make up their own minds, based on a one to one relationship with a supplier, and hardly ever follow the purchasing recommendation of a secretariat.

Dealing with a group involves a huge cost in confidentiality. Sensitive price lists will practically become the public domain, as well as discount policies and various forms of promotional support which are critically confidential between supplier and distributor. During the group's conferences and junkets, product performance and important sales statistics will be freely and carelessly exchanged. Sometimes this can be good in that one dealer's success with a particular product might rub off on some of the others and inspire them to greater efforts. Sadly, however, the bad news is usually shared first since their first motive will be to protect and excuse themselves – so they will likely concentrate on product failures rather than successes!

Dealing with purchasing groups can lead to unwelcome restrictions and complications when one later tries to refine one's distribution machine. Effectively there can be too many eggs in one basket. What once seemed a magic wand in opening up national sales potential can become an obstructive monster when trying to expand a dealership.

Finally, on this score, while dealer groups are not favoured, they are not always to be dismissed. In Germany, for example, because there are many of them, there will be other baskets to run to if relationships with one or two of them sour. In other words, you will have the protection of competition. Again, some countries such as Australia pose enormous logistical problems in distribution due to the geography and demographics – so groups have emerged which purchase centrally for redistribution to affiliates in far-flung areas, and these groups do represent real opportunities for market entry. However, what we have said about later complication when modifying distribution channels still applies!

The selection process is relatively easy when one has done the preparatory work well and has clear goals in filling slots in a well-defined plan. In this chapter we have concentrated on auditing and qualifying those who seem to fit our plans. Hopefully the result will be, for an individual territory, a company – or series of companies – which will dovetail with the distribution model that we have selected and which is sufficiently equipped and motivated to do the job that we require of it.

Normally this means an adequate and qualified sales force sensibly distributed throughout the territory involved. It means acceptable back-up at head office by way of sales management, marketing management, product management and service facilities. You will have easy access to the company, from management through to the individual sales staff, so that you can be involved deeply in the sales and market planning and achieve the vital product and sales training throughout the organisation. Management, from the outset, will be genuinely interested in your product and motivated to make a success of it in their company. This will be supported by a realistic attitude towards inventory and a satisfactory commitment in terms of promotional resources and access to their selling organisation. More simply – they will make their sales staff available to you for training at headquarters and in the field, and are prepared to cough up money for a respectable stocking order and for a reasonable package of advertising, exhibiting, mailing, sampling and other promotional activities. And the company will be strong enough financially to provide all these services without fiscal strain and to pay their bills on time.

5

Contracting

Once a line has been established internationally and has proven its market acceptance and profit potential, franchising will be very much a seller's market, and more and more time and skill can be devoted to the refinement of the distribution system and to screening component partners. In the early days, however, securing the interest and services of active distributors will probably be a serious selling challenge.

OK, we have to choose mechanisms, we have to select partners, dealers, agents who we consider will fit the bill and get the job done for us. Having made our selection, however, the ball will in many cases fall on the other foot and we will be faced with the considerable task of convincing these people to run with our product.

Honeymoon

Remember, from earlier discussions, that dealers instinctively bid for all franchises initially and run with them, toy with them or reject them later – at their leisure and discretion. This phenomenon is responsible for the famous honeymoon phase which invariably accompanies the early stages of discussion between a new supplier and a seasoned distributor. During first contacts a prospective dealer will simply be bidding for the option of handling one's line, and he will draw upon all the necessary skill and enthusiasm to see that he is successful in winning this option. His aggressiveness and posture will be indistinguishable from one who is genuinely interested in the line. Less experienced suppliers will usually then return to base intoxicated from skilful sales pitches by the distributor, and naturally flattered by their quick success in winning interest and forging a warm but illusory relationship. There will be the memories of testing but positive meetings with myriad senior managers, the honour of a prestigious luncheon with the company chairman, the savoured sharing of confidential future corporate structures and sensitive staffing data and the warmth and humour of long dinners and good brandy. The actual situation will usually only emerge much later and painfully when, in the more obvious cases, promised follow-up items fail to materialise, correspondence and telefaxes go unanswered and appointments fall through. Sometimes it may be more subtle, for example relegation of your affairs to an underling or deferment of the project on the pretext of needed market studies.

In most cases a really new entrant to the market will need to be carefully sold to a suitable partner, and love at first sight rarely occurs. The trick is to learn to recognise mirages early, before they waste time and effort. One of the few real values of a contract is as a screening tool, but before dealing with this closing device we need to look at some ways of enhancing our approaching pitch.

Changing Times

To be fair to distributors in general, they really do need to have thick skins when making franchise selections. Running a distribution business is certainly not the easiest way of making a living for most. Good distributors fight a constant battle to keep focus in their companies and to avoid unprofitable diversifications, or ones which would distract from and undermine their core businesses. In older and less competitive times, big old distribution companies would treat agencies like collectors' items and think nothing of handling the businesses of thirty major principals and hosts of smaller ones. Their catalogues could have up to 60,000 items and all of these were expected to be sold by a handful of veteran salesmen.

Of course these poor salesmen could not be expected to really know their products, much less to actually detail and sell them. So they became so-called 'order-takers', expecting the actual customer to catch them on their rounds and to specify his requirements! These houses were lord of all but master of none. They wanted to be regarded as total suppliers, as one-stop shops. They hated the idea of a customer going to another shop, so their policy was to stock everything to avoid losing him. They may have kept the customers, but they rarely had a satisfied principal and they began to lose these as suppliers discovered that focused marketing and selling brought them greater market shares than being in the town emporium. Products became more technically sophisticated and had shorter cycles. While they offered great profits, they could not simply be advertised or catalogued – they needed to be demonstrated and sold through by salespeople who knew what they were doing.

For these and many more reasons, distributors learned to focus on much tighter ranges of products and to look for profits through specialisation and bigger, more controlled market shares. Done well, this brought not only customer loyalty but also supplier loyalty from satisfied individual principals. They thus became tougher and much more discerning in adding lines.

The Fantasy

Again, in fairness to dealers, they have to spend a lot of time fending off bad products, simplistic people and often downright crackpots. Every minute of the day, somewhere, someone is inventing a new widget or fantasising about vastly profitable expansions into export markets. In attics, parlours and offices the naïve are daily bent over maps and statistics, making apparently conservative extrapolations of sales potential based on populations and other statistical economic and political data. The fantasy will climax with a modern-day Don Quixote astride a commercial jet, scouring the globe for those converts who will bring him the dream – effortless sales globally at no risk and minimum investment. This is really not an enormous exaggeration. Backers and financiers, studying business plans and profit and loss projections, find it relatively easy to check lower elements in the P and L such as labour and material costs, sales expenses, factory overheads, administration and so forth. The most critical element in a new business projection is most often the sales projection. While most other elements can be tweaked and adjusted, without the sales there is no profit and no cash-flow. Yet paradoxically the sales projection is usually the one taken most on faith and least subject to effective scrutiny. Decisions are made on simple price-performance studies against competitors and, critically, on the assumption that a few positive gauge readings on the product will be sufficient to galvanise herds of distributors in action. Then, according to the fantasy, all that will be needed are some samples, a credit card, some brochures, a few exhibitions and six weeks' selective globetrotting.

To the contrary, once a good distributor has been found it will be no mean task, in most cases, to convince him that your product can bring him profitable and significant incremental business within a reasonable period of time, and that it will represent a good investment for him in staff time and inventory without a cost to any of his valuable existing lines.

Sheer Selling

In order to achieve this, good selling techniques and routines will be necessary. All the basics of probing, filling needs and effective closing will be required. Put simply, it is a selling job and requires as much preparation, training and rehearsal as does the actual selling of the product. Mistakes are so often made here, when people perfectly capable of general management or market analysis but poorly qualified in selling are dispatched to close deals with distributors. This is often mistakenly done on the assumption that managers had better deal with managers, owners with owners. Now the dealer owner is probably a skilled salesman since he's in the distribution business – but the managing director from the supplier could well be an accountant or a physicist, and not at all up to the challenge. Such people should be involved only in the later stages, when the deal is effectively struck and when all that is left is largely ceremonial.

Selling distributors on concepts and negotiating franchises is a finely tuned and complex affair involving webs of counter-argument, dissimulation and quid pro quo. There is nothing more shattering for a skilled negotiator than the earlier intrusion of a senior but untutored executive tearing the whole fabric of the negotiation apart with mistimed frankness, pre-emptive disclosures and general indiscretion. No amount of briefing will compensate for these skills or adequately prepare one of these people for the equally skilled probing of the distributor, and their premature involvement will be not unlike inviting audience participation in a performance of *La Traviata.*

So the approach to the dealer should be handled with professional selling skills and all the appropriate trappings of an effective sales pitch, such as a well-prepared and smooth presentation routine, supportive data and illustrations, slick product displays and adequate literature, catalogues and other impressive pieces. There are some other key ingredients.

Phantoms

Never allow a distributor to think it's a one-horse race. First, it isn't. Just because he's your clear first preference does not mean he is the last option. Just because you haven't yet found another option does not mean they don't exist. Therefore you're not really being dishonest. If a competitive distributor does not yet exist, then create one! Flesh one out in your mind, convince yourself he exists, and then allow this illusion to influence your attitude to your real prospect. On ethical grounds you can never be forced to name your phantom.

Never allow your target dealer to pick you up at the airport. Arrive a day early, catch up on some paperwork and call around noon a day later. Imply that you had other appointments! Allude frequently and with familiarity to other distribution houses and particularly to ones in competitive areas. Carry their literature, business cards and corporate profiles loosely in your briefcase. If the opportunity presents itself, be seen spending time at other dealers' booths at trade shows, preferably emerging from back rooms or going for morning coffee.

Whether the competitor for your line is real or imaginary, he will be essential in underpinning your value to the real target. We have only to look at our own lives to see how we depend on the opinions of others to make our own appraisals. To the contrary, without this competitive element you may well take on the appearance of a pariah or, at the least, an unsafe bet.

Appearances

Despite all the best advice, books continue to be judged by their covers. A professional salesman will know how to dress and how to present himself. But his supportive materials must also be up to standard. If budgets are tight then skimp, initially, on the range of supports but not the quality. Use photocopied product manuals, skip the corporate brochure, cut out mailing pieces and printed price lists but have at least one piece, such as brochure or catalogue, done in first-class full-colour quality.

For initial meetings at least, stay at good hotels. While the Shangri-La is not always necessary, the impression and doubts caused by one's tattered emergence from the Chung Wei Guest House are not worth the savings involved. Neither does a thrifty upbringing or ultra-conservative corporate spending policy carry much weight with people, or in countries, where status, influence and value are expected by custom to be reflected in certain standards of life-style. Later on, when relationships are consolidated, eccentricity or conservatism won't matter. But why confuse the issue, at an early stage, with a private crusade for thrift?

These considerations are clearly more important in some areas than others and would be less of an issue in the United States or in New Zealand than, for example, in France or in Japan, where the selection of accommodation would weigh seriously in an assessment.

There are other ways of improving appearances at little cost. Certain hotels and airlines offer business facilities and small conference rooms very reasonably. These are infinitely better meeting places than an odorous or claustrophobic hotel bedroom. Overseas branches of National Export Boards or Departments of Trade and Commerce usually have excellent facilities for meetings at the best addresses and can often also be counted on for lavish entertainment!

Specifics

If your prospective distributor is a good businessman, the foremost questions on his mind will be potential sales volumes, profit margins, investment in stock, compatibility with his existing activities and after-sales service requirements. He is unlikely to be so orderly in his probing, however, and his concerns will manifest themselves in questions about sales in other countries, special prices, competitive pricing, support for advertising and promotional programmes, deferred payment on opening stocking order and details of your own service facilities. Allowing the distributor to extract the information from you and to paint his own picture, willy-nilly, is the wrong way to sell a programme. Be prepared with specifics to answer his critical concerns and pre-empt as many as possible.

Produce a sales scenario, by product, for his first year. Draw upon the data you accumulated when you analysed the territory and during the selection process. Make it conservative but attractive. Check that it poses a relatively modest target for each of his salesmen and show these as easily obtainable monthly quotas. You will be surprised how quickly ultra-modest weekly sales quotas can gross up to really interesting figures!

Help the dealer to visualise his market and give him a matrix of potential outlets for the principal products; specify the retail possibilities, identify the specialty market, talk about government business, potential with the military, OEM opportunities, private labelling possibilities, and so forth. It is here that all the groundwork done with customers when choosing the mechanism, and when qualifying your dealers, will be of enormous benefit. You will be able to allude freely and confidently to customers on his patch, their positive reactions to your products and to make extrapolations from these factual experiences to support the sales figures you've projected. That groundwork done in the market establishes the vital credibility needed to give him confidence in making sales.

Preparation is also needed on the question of profitability. Keep calculators and confusion to a minimum with well-prepared gross margin studies. No two people look at margins the same way, and discussions can become chaotic with one group talking 'mark-up', another talking gross margin, confusion between retail and net prices, and so on. Work up some examples and don't be simplistic. Factor in the inevitable discounts and deals that make the world go round. Cater for lower tender prices and bulk discounting. Pitch your suggested selling prices realistically and don't inflate the values of marginal benefits in your products. Make allowances in your pricing for sales to sub-distributors and for any agent commissions where these might apply. Critically make provision for inevitable currency fluctuations. If this is all done well, and if we remember the fundamentals, the essential motivation, your projections will boil down to an attractive average gross margin. More on this later.

It is not wise at this stage to be too specific about stocking requirements. Best to keep this discussion for now to principles. Define the products which he will market. Agree certain stocking policies first. For instance, for most non-capital items this policy might be that the dealer should carry inventories which would be, at all times, compatible with offering your equipment ex-stock to customers in his territory. For higher-value capital equipment it might be to hold one demonstration unit and one inventory back-up unit for each of your major products. Details should be deferred until you have had access to more of the sales staff and executives and the opportunity to generate support for the line more widely in the company. The task of agreeing opening inventory is vastly more simple when you have the commitment and the support of the sales team. With their support and an agreed policy, a healthy stocking order will follow as a natural consequence.

If your product is not a good fit with the dealer's other lines, then the chances are that you have made a bad selection. If they do fit reasonably well you may still have a problem in persuading the distributor that the inevitable distraction which a new line causes will not adversely impact his established lines. So be modest in your initial demands for training time and concentrate on projecting your product as a door opener, as an incremental sale, as a natural adjunct which demands little extra time and thus contributes greatly to the bottom line. And, as is likely entering a new market, if your arrangements for service and repair are not too clear then at least be prepared to discuss options such as repair on his premises, an independent service contractor, a float system to allow factory repairs and so forth. It should be side-stepped as a detail but not as a concern.

Misconceptions

A distributor contract is one of the most over-rated and falsely perceived documents dealt with in international business. Time and again executives fall into the trap of ascribing intrinsic value to this trading agreement between distributor and supplier. In a way this is understandable. The darned things are so unreadable, so difficult to follow, devour so much time and polemic, cost so much by way of legal fees, that it is probably only natural to feel that they must be valuable!

If your goal is to sell product, be clear that a dealer contract will not achieve this. A dealer will sell only if he's motivated, if there is significant sales potential, if there are good profits, if there is compatibility, if there is balance in the relationship, if he needs your product as a corollary to others. No piece of paper, no clause, no lawyer will force him to work for your product if he is not motivated.

Often, dealer contracts seem to have generated business. For example, they may often include agreed levels for opening stocking orders, or they may include annual purchases targets. These inclusions give the document an illusion of currency, of value. The point is that neither the stocking order, nor the annual agreed level of purchases, will be reached unless the dealer wants to, and three tons of legal documentation will make no difference. While this may seem obvious to some, it is extraordinary how often an export sales manager will triumphantly flourish a contract and suggest a drink to celebrate what he sees as finished business.

The more seasoned know that you can drag a horse to water but you can't make him drink, and that the last thing that document guarantees is a stock order or ongoing sales. In essence a contract with a distributor is little more than a termination document. If a distributor wants to perform well for your company it is because he wants to retain the franchise – not because there is a contract. If he honours territory boundaries it is because he doesn't want to jeopardise the relationship. If he sticks to agreed pricing levels, if he provides certain service facilities, if he refrains from selling competitive products, if he provides market data, then he does all this because, and only because, he doesn't want to lose the line. The moment he doesn't care, the moment he stops performing – then you will want to change or terminate his franchise and then, and only then, does the contract become important.

The Contract

A well-prepared and effective contract will first arm the supplier with a multitude of reasons for terminating and, second, protect the supplier during and after termination – just that. It will have scores of reasons by which to judge a contract breached, and full and adequate protection for the principal when he chooses to invoke one or several of these. When completed and agreed, it will be put to bed and forgotten about until that day when the supplier decides that his network needs changing.

It may also be useful for protecting the supplier from public, product and warranty liabilities in each country – although this can be accomplished in other, simpler ways.

Therefore look upon a contract as a series of clauses whereupon you can nail your distributor in the event that you decide he is no longer suitable, and a further series of clauses to allow a smooth and danger-free termination.

PERFORMANCE: Define what you mean in volume terms. The contract does not have to be predicated on this figure, but you do need to ballpark a number around which performance can be roughly judged. So there should be provision for an agreed annual sales performance figure which would constitute acceptable performance. While this will be a grey area, at least an arbitrator will have a yardstick on performance expectations.

ACTIVITIES: Take the trouble to specify the kind of activity which you expect in representing your products: ongoing detailing; sales evaluations; trade shows and exhibitions; advertising; mailings; promotional activities; use of literature; production of local language literature; participation in government tenders, and so on. Take the time to include the types of market areas and customer groups which you expect to see covered. And define what you mean by coverage. Don't leave it loose. If you mean actual sales calls and demonstrations, then say so. Be as quantitative as possible – list known essential trade shows and define what you mean by attendance. Specify the actual journals and the type of advertising which you envisage. Schedule those key customers and decision makers which are important and how they should be handled. If this dreadful document is going to be done at all it should be done well. As the expression goes: 'Don't sink the ship for a ha'p'orth of tar!'

LAUNCHING: You know it will take a special effort to get your product off the ground, so specify this effort; seminars for key customer groups; evaluations with system specialists and key decision makers and industry leaders; launch exhibitions; launch advertising, detailing, mailing and the like.

INVENTORIES: The priority here is to include the agreed formula for stocking. This is usually best phrased by reference to the type of deliveries which end-users should expect. This clause represents an ideal opportunity also to come to grips with the issue of the opening stock order. Try to have the value of the stocking order included in this clause or appended to the contract.

PERSONNEL: List the teams or staff that are expected to be deployed in the sale of your product and clarify any specialist staff or product managers that have been promised, with the portions of their time which have been pledged. This is an excellent trapping clause. Remember that most dealers will pledge practically anything to get a valued franchise, including full-time product managers, entire sales teams and even the lavatory cleaners, if necessary. Hold them to their promises in this clause and hoard this condition for future use.

TRAINING: Quantify what you mean by reasonable access to staff for training purposes and establish your right to conduct this training also in the field. If your product proves reasonably active you won't normally have trouble in participating at sales meetings for training purposes – but field work can become a sticky issue, particularly with managers who fear intrusion and distraction or with resentful salesmen.

INFORMATION: State that data which you expect to be made freely available to you and at what intervals: sales statistics, territory analysis, sales/marketing plans, inventory levels, competitive data and so forth. Remember the mushroom principle! Data on customers, current sales prospects, sales levels and inventories are jealously guarded by dealers. Yet this data will be vital to you, on a regular basis, for building forecasts, controlling production and lessening your umbilical relationship with the dealer.

EXCLUSIVITY: Can the dealer handle competitive products? Can you supply other dealers in the same territory? Is the exclusive right by region or by product sector or by market sector? The question of exclusivity is one of the thorniest issues in distribution. Naturally the distributor wants the maximum amount of exclusivity that he can get. If the project proves too much for him he can always sub-distribute or hive the pressure off in some other way. Above all, however, he wants to control these issues. He does not want to see a principal engaged in incestuous relationships with other companies. He will not want odious performance comparisons or to be pushed into rat-races with his competitors. There is the question of loss of face from a shared franchise. He has legitimate fears of other companies pirating his customers. Arguments about carefully controlled territory boundaries and market sector protection will be little comfort to him. He himself will be an expert in claim-jumping and will expect no less from his competitors!

The supplier, on the other hand, will be reluctant to part with exclusivity. Even if the mechanism he has chosen allows exclusivity he will still want the flexibility to expand and change as time goes on. The catch, of course, is that suppliers usually want monogamous dealers and will consider swapping exclusivity to get it. And remember that they are also infinitely better served through well motivated dealers – not ones who are nervous or uncommitted!

TERRITORY: Define it, who is to share it, what the relationships are with main importers or other elements in your sales set-up.

PRODUCT: Carefully specify the products. Who knows how your company may diversify in the future and the different channels that might be needed for radically new products? Make sure any new products, which would be significantly different from current ones, are negotiable.

SUB-DISTRIBUTION: Be sure to reserve the right to veto sub-distributors, some of whom may want to buy your products for the wrong reasons, perhaps for resale to a different territory or to get access to pricing information for a competitor.

PRICING: Prices should be appended but with the minimum impact on confidentiality – so keep high volume discounts off the agenda at this time. Discount schedules should be clear and geared to encourage efficient shipments. Standardise on FOB factory prices and protect yourself for insurance and bank charges connected with shipments. Ensure your right to change prices without notice. While you will customarily want to give reasonable notice of price change, you must protect yourself against error or traumatic increases in manufacturing costs.

PAYMENT: Internationally this will be one of the most effective termination clauses, as dealers rarely stick to payment terms, so be specially clear on the mode of payment and the precise credit terms.

RETURNS: A particularly important clause. Any termination will raise the spectre of returns for credit, so it is vital to make returns fully discretionary on the supplier's part and to define rules in connection with the costs of transhipment, any necessary refurbishment, obsolescence, methods of shipment, associated declarations and credit values.

PERIOD: Generally manufacturers want flexibility and therefore look for the shortest possible contract period. Distributors, on the other hand, will be fretting about the black widow syndrome and will want the maximum possible as a token of security. The trick is to strike a balance here where a distributor can be relaxed but not complacent. Anyhow, if a contract is well peppered with terminated clauses, and provided the term of the contract is clearly related to fulfilment of obligations, there should be no problem in extrication. Termination notice will need to be specified and this, again, negotiated to a minimum.

CHANGES: Contracts should be protected against changes in business ownership. While such changes often make little difference, or may even be positive, there is always the hazard of purchase by a competitor or other company with conflicting interests.

MARKET DEVELOPMENT: This is an awfully important clause, particularly in the litigious countries. When a distribution partnership unilaterally ruptures it is not unlike a broken marriage. Bitterness sets in and pretty soon the wounded party starts thinking in abstracts. He remembers all the time and sweat put into developing the market for your products and establishing your brand with customers. Pretty soon he starts to impute a value to all this effort, this goodwill which he helped create. The next step can be a massive claim for reimbursement for so-called market development costs. While you might successfully fight off such a claim, the litigation, at the very least, will be used as an excuse for non-payment of invoices due or maybe as a refusal to return samples or exhibiting materials which were on loan.

Concessions

To this point we have dealt only with clauses which protect the supplier – which is fine, since this is the priority. But a contract must at least appear to be balanced and fair or your target dealer is going to have psychological problems. So take those basic items which you are going to have to do anyway as a serious supplier, and turn them into concessionary offerings from the principal.

You will be supplying literature, catalogues, mailing pieces, product manuals, posters, sales demonstration equipment. You will be planning special training seminars for dealer staff – and inviting certain key personnel to your facilities for more in-depth training. Field-work with dealer sales staff will be essential. Contributions are going to be made in time and money terms to major trade shows, exhibitions, promotion and advertising – at the very least by way of artwork, copy and show materials. Repair, maintenance and product warranty programmes will be inevitable. And, usually at any rate, you will also be conceding some sort of exclusivity or voluntary restriction. So take all these and any other such items and, with reasonably skilled use of the pen, turn them into sacrificial clauses in the distributor's favour and disperse them through the contract document.

No contract will be either complete or safe until you have thrown it over to the legal eagles to perform their voodoo. Many of them will have little grasp of the commercial significance of the clauses which you have drafted but they can at least check them for any obvious legal heresy. They start to be useful when it comes to including protective clauses in respect of limitations of warranty, product liability, non-disclosure, consequential damages resulting from breach of contract, product registrations, patents and so forth. Finally, of course, their most important function is to ensure that the contract is either enforceable or totally useless in a particular country, depending on your needs.

The necessity for a contract varies enormously from country to country. In fact, in many cases an actual legal contract is a waste of time. They are unenforceable from the dealer's point of view and, as we've said, over and over, are of no value in actually generating sales. They do, however, bring a valuable air of gravity and solemnity into a new commercial relationship, and the sense of occasion generated is another valuable tool in extracting nice opening stock orders! Furthermore, contracts serve as a useful and permanent statement of policy. They are, in effect, charters of mutual expectation and an excellent reference when chiding, warning or actually terminating a distributor. A contract can be a type of permanent rule book which can cut out a lot of useless argument and polemic – a sort of constitution, to be referred to as final arbitrator when all else fails.

Finally, in a growing number of countries, contracts are either mandated by law or are, in any case, vital in order to protect the supplier. Some countries, such as Germany, have long since legislated heavily in favour of an agent or distributor – particularly when there is no protective contract in place. This tendency has spread to France, Italy and others, and with the growth and consolidation of the European Community it will soon be the rule in Western Europe. Here the allowable procedures for termination are very precise. A poor contract and a messy termination can have a huge cost, not only in consequential claims from the injured party, but also from lost time, lost sales and legal expenses. Also the very emergence of the European Community has raised complications for the control of supply channels. For example, one cannot any longer restrict a sales territory legally. There is no way to prevent a French distributor from buying one's product in Belgium. This opens up the spectre of parallel distribution and makes the protection of territories, and therefore of franchises, very difficult.

Clearly, nowadays the fail-safe position would be to instigate a distributor contract in all cases, irrespective of the individual circumstances. As mentioned, this will be mandatory in some cases, particularly in developing countries and in the Gulf states where governments are increasingly insisting on distribution contracts, not to protect the national distributor, but in fact to protect the final customer or end-user of the product. These countries have had their fingers burned repeatedly by fly-by-night operators, particularly those in capital equipment, who have made big and fast bucks importing high-technology equipment but making no satisfactory service or maintenance arrangements. Many a factory, oilfield, military base, hospital and school has been left with an expensive but useless hunk of equipment rusting for the want of a spare part – and in the more extreme cases, user training!

Although most of these mandatory contracts are designed to protect the customer from the dealer, they are usually quite draconian and severe on the supplier and contain clauses in respect of supplier liability and exposure that would make any corporate lawyer blanch. Worse, they are seldom negotiable. The government involved takes the simple but effective stance that if one wants to do business in, say, Saudi Arabia, then sign – otherwise move aside. In these cases there are three choices. Try to negotiate the problematic clauses; indemnify your company some way, perhaps through self-insurance, against negative consequences; or conduct your business through a third, but offshore, party, who will buffer or totally absorb the exposure.

All in all, contracts are, then, an inevitable fact of life, at times a mandatory hurdle, more usually a necessary prophylactic in adealer relationship. They are a useful reference for the ground rules during disputes. They are, however, bills of expectations, and are rarely commercially significant, in the important sense of generating business. Their really key functions will be to smooth changes in the distribution mechanism and to make terminations quick and painless.

6

INITIATION

Looking at initiation as a separate entity might well seem, to some, to be too analytical, and the pragmatist might well say: 'Heck, just let's get on with the job!' Unfortunately, in too many cases, a horrible anticlimax is allowed to develop after the more exciting days of hooking and contracting a good dealer who fits well with the master distribution plan.

Hiatus

First, far too much intelligence, professonalism and enthusiasm is ascribed to the distributor. Time and again the contract or handshake is thought to be a starting pistol, and the supplier lies back in an exhausted post-coital slumber dreaming of legions of dealer salesmen swarming all over the territory detailing product and booking orders. Nothing could be further from the truth. Although some stocking product may have been ordered, you and your products have probably been totally forgotten – if not by management, then certainly by the salespeople. Those salespeople that you met have since shaken themselves out of the trance and woken up to the reality of trying to deal with ten other major lines and 15,000 products.

Even those salesmen who were impressed and seemed anxious to run with your line only retained about 8 per cent of the information you put across during your product presentation, and they would feel hopelessly inept and insecure about demonstrations at this stage. Furthermore, they would probably have only a hazy idea where to go with your products. They would have little idea how they stack up against the competition. Sales and marketing management have also only a notional idea of the range, features and benefits of your products and where they can be sold. Your product codes and price lists are probably totally confusing to them, and the samples and product manuals which you left with them have more than likely been locked away in the product manager's cabinet – never to see the light of day again.

The proprietor has possibly gone totally cold on the idea of the franchise. He has had time to become negative, and those inevitable people in his company who opposed the whole idea have had time to work on him and feed his anxieties.

Those who don't implement a specific initiation phase will smell a rat when the invoice for the stocking order goes into a black hole and, for one reason or another, doesn't get paid. Worse, if the opening stock was consigned on sight draft it might lie in some bonded warehouse for months, uncollected, and with mounting demurrage costs. There may be some correspondence suggesting that the discounts offered are hopelessly inadequate. Once distributors have lost enthusiasm they will deploy an apparently inexhaustible stream of negatives – prices will be queried, there will be suggestions of double-dealing and availability of your products through competitors, clauses in the contract will be queried all over, competitive aspects of the product will be challenged, the quality of the samples will be criticised and loose service arrangements will be cited as reasons for inactivity. If all else fails they will fall back on 'timing' and defer the entire launch to coincide with some distant trade fair or congress.

These sorts of signals take time to read, and when the message has finally filtered through relationships will probably be irreparably damaged. Usually the dealer gets blamed, but in fact it is largely the fault of the supplier. He has made the mistake of assuming that a handshake, a contract and a modest stocking order means a commitment. In fact, as we have concluded already, it means little more than that the distributor has purchased an option for himself, and could even, in some cases, be a calculated red herring.

Closing

An initiation phase is really the final closing device, the one that takes your chosen representative beyond the dabbling stage and into the realm of real and tangible commitment to your company and your equipment – one from which he cannot easily withdraw and one from which he later will not wish to withdraw provided your researchers and your product are valid.

While initiation is mostly active and practical – training, pricing, stocking and so forth – it has one enormous abstract benefit which makes it the most powerful of all closing tools. If it is well planned, proprietors and senior management will be deeply involved in the planning meetings, the launch sales meetings, press releases, launch advertising and so on. In this way they will be giving a deep and public commitment to the project and one which will almost always ensure that the franchise will get a fair crack of the whip – at least for the vital first twelve months! So when, in this chapter, we talk about some of the elements in initiation and launching, always keep at the back of your mind the parallel purpose of selling through a new idea and of preserving the impetus and support right through a distributor organisation from top to bottom.

This process is usually shrugged off on the basis of the time available. Over and over again exporters swing into Hong Kong calling on Jardine, Goodman, Yung Hung Hong and Golden Mile Enterprises, and go through all the rituals of product presentation, management meetings, Peking duck and nightcaps at the Meridian. Then probably on to Taipei to meet twenty more merchant princes and take part in a drinking marathon. Singapore is probably next, armed with fistfuls of leads from the department of commerce, embassies or trade missions – a lot more talking and a lot more drinking. It is not unusual for the expedition to continue on down to Auckland and then over to Sydney and Melbourne. The point is that most of these visits will be wasted unless there is time and provision also for the vital follow-up to initiate. There's little point in lighting twenty wet squibs throughout Asia – although that is often done in the hope that, by spreading the net, one or two will take off. In fact, the percentage play is to limit the number of territories opened so that new dealerships can be properly initiated and worked on a continuous basis.

This can be tough medicine for a lone export manager who is under pressure from the factory to bring in orders – those retainer orders are very tempting, and it takes discipline to keep the big picture in mind and ensure that time is available to follow up the priority hits and to initiate fully. And experience shows that initiation has to be a specific and well-timed programme and will rarely happen on its own as a natural progression.

Pick Winners

For a wide product range, the first discussion should centre on which products to focus on during launch of the line and all the related pricing and discount structures. More on pricing later, but clearly it doesn't make sense to dilute the initial effort over too many products.

Nor does it make a lot of sense, at the early stages, to insist on a detailed sales plan for the first year. Better, more relevant plans will emerge as a result of launching experience. Good field-work during the study and selection phases will help enormously to steer initial effort into productive areas, but the approach should still be fairly open-minded until the dealer sales team gets a chance to get its feet wet. These are critical days and it is so important that the distributor salesman get to taste success early and not rejection. In the beginning, motivation and encouragement of a novice sales team is vital – it is no time for beating the bushes or taking on fringe areas where the business is difficult to get. You want those salesmen cutting orders and making commission on your product as soon as possible, so pick targets where you know this is most likely to happen; and if you don't know, then at least give them the room to experiment and find out for themselves.

Novelty

Don't squander promotions such as special discounts or other deals during launch. First, the product is new to the sales force and probably new to the market, so it is self-promoting by virtue of its novelty. Good salespeople don't need an incentive to test a new product, and special offers on first approaches to customers would smack of prostitution. Nonetheless, distributors will ask for concessions, even during launch. They do this to test a new principal – a sort of muscle-flexing exercise to let a new supplier know that prices are not sacrosanct and will be continually challenged. Being salesmen, of course, they also want the easy way out and know that a specially low price certainly won't hurt. It's extremely important to resist these inevitable early overtures for price concessions and to signal a new dealer that your price lists and discounts are serious – even if they are not. So launch activities should really focus on exposure and not concession.

Literature

Good literature pieces will need to be prepared, but with an open mind, since these will probably need a change in emphasis as trends emerge. Therefore demands should be conservative at the beginning and should focus on overview pieces and cataloguing. Whether or not these pieces need translation is an endless topic. Clearly the optimum is to have all literature in all the active local languages. Equally clearly this is not always financially possible or desirable. It will, however, be essential in Japan and highly desirable in Germany, France, Italy, Korea, mainland China, Taiwan and the Spanish-speaking countries. English has wide acceptance in Scandinavia, the Benelux countries, India and Pakistan and, generally, in South East Asia. So the batting order for literature language is English first, followed by Japanese, French, German and Spanish, provided, of course, that one is launching in these territories.

Exposure

Congresses, exhibitions and trade fairs will be key launching platforms. While their value should rightly always be subject to scrutiny, there is no question of the effectiveness of shows to announce a presence in the marketplace. Where the customer base is very broad these shows will be the only cost-effective way of getting to large groups of customers or to dispersed retail groups.

Needless to say, advertising and mailing to targeted groups are proven ways to launch. If the customer base is not too wide, a mailing is easier to sell to a distributor, since mailing responses usually represent well-qualified sales leads whereas journal advertising usually has a high spiritual element to it and the rewards are not immediately so palpable. Generally speaking, distributors are very wary of advertising, precisely because they perpetually have difficulty in quantifying its value. So if a supplier is convinced that he needs journal advertising for profile purposes, then he is probably going to have to come up with a decent contribution towards costs to get it going. If journal or press advertising is being planned, then of course every opportunity should be grasped for press release and the free editorial space which publications offer to lure advertisers.

If the customer base is highly focused, as with highly specialised industrial capital equipment, government supplies or medical specialty equipment, then a whole host of additional launch vehicles can be considered, including sponsorship of specialty groups and events and highly effective seminars on related topics.

Low Profile

All of this assumes that publicity is desirable and that one is going for the maximum profile possible within reasonable costs. This is not always the case. It is often much better to get a lot of groundwork done in the market before alerting competitors to a new arrival or a change in distribution. Competitors are usually credited with far too much intelligence. Competitors' dealers suffer from just the same weaknesses as our own. Their salesmen, too, grossly exaggerate their contact with the market and their product managers are just as distracted and over-worked. It can often take months before they wake up to a competitor. During that time much can be accomplished to swing customers on to a better product. So a firework display during the earlier stages of a launch can often be counter-productive, giving your competitors all sorts of opportunity to pre-empt your first strike with negative publicity and creative pricing and promotions. One has to weigh these dangers against the need to inform, and generally this decision is closely tied to the size of the customer base. The more compact the target, the easier it will be to launch on a low profile. If one is selling recycling machines for waste paper, then a full launch can prob-ably be conducted quietly and thoroughly to all the decision-makers in a matter of weeks. A laboratory weighing scale, however, needs exposure and will benefit little from silence.

Teaching

Probably the best way to underwrite the success of a new line within a dealership is through training. This is so important and so fundamental that we will treat it separately. The point is that it is an ongoing perpetual basic of success with distributors, and never as important as at the beginning.

It is training that will bring you into your first intimate contact with the dealer sales force. At this time these salespeople will use the opportunity to judge you and your company and to form vital first impressions which will directly govern the subsequent amount of time, if any, that they will devote to your line. A lacklustre, careless, unprofessional, unhelpful and even boring initial training will strangle a product at birth – guaranteed, If, on the other hand, training is well done, it will arm the salesman with the confidence and familiarity which he needs to sell the product. If it is exceptionally well done, it will go an enormous way towards that key fundamental objective of diverting sales time from the other product lines on to yours! Books are still judged by their covers, and an exceptional training will enormously enhance a dealer salesman's impression of your company and products and make life an awful lot easier when discussing tricky price and performance questions later.

In addition to the normal training skills, the initial training commands special treatment. There must not be overkill, rather it should be edited down and centred on those products chosen for focus during launch; absolutely no assumptions should be made about the intelligence, experience or knowledge of the audience; while at its core it must be informative, it should also be interesting, enjoyable and not too difficult. It should be presented not as a one-shot deal, but as part of an ongoing process with milestones, checkpoints and performance evaluations; there must be opportunity to establish one-on-one relationships with the sales team; and it should encompass not only product training, but market training and actual selling skills.

We will try to explain how all this can practically be done, but it is self-evident that whoever does the training needs to be properly qualified and, sadly, this is one of the commonest omissions in international sales effort. The fact of the matter is that a successful international salesman, or sales manager, is also, in large measure, a teacher and needs excellent communication skills.

The training requirement also varies, depending on the audience. If senior management attend portions of the meeting for their general information, then this had better be recognised and that section of the training suitably adapted. They will need to see the products in clearer competitive perspective, in terms of market potential, in terms of profitability and in terms of 'fit' with other lines. For the general sales force the training will focus on features and sales opportunities, while the engineering and technical groups will want to get right into manuals, systems and detailed technical applications.

Man Friday

Of course, that key individual selected as sales specialist or product manager needs very special treatment. His training needs to be very broad and very deep. The product specialist is possibly the most important potential asset in any distribution company. Looking back over a wide variety of businesses, if there is a common denominator in successful franchises it is that a certain individual within the dealership became closely, personally and enthusiastically involved in the line. This feature qualifies as a true fundamental. This flag-carrier for your line in a busy dealership can be your eyes and ears in the long months between visits. He or she will be specially trained and equipped to handle the day-to-day plethora of detailed queries on product and application. The product specialist will be the one, in your absence, to drive the annual sales and marketing plan. The product specialist will implement and push product promotions and new product launches through the sales team. Irrespective of computer inventory systems, the product specialist will be the real driving force behind inventory policies and, as a result, orders. The product specialist is the one who sees to it that samples are ordered, demonstration equipment kept available and in good condition, and stocks of literature, mailers, posters, advertisement pulls and the like kept up to date. The product specialist will take care of key and demanding customers and opinion leaders with the personal contact and deeper product knowledge which they demand. He ensures that, within the dealership, you get at least your fair share of booth space at exhibitions, display areas in the showrooms and illustration and copy in general distributor catalogues.

All of this may sound like a pipe-dream. There are obstacles. Although all these functions are eminently justifiable, dealers will usually fight this sort of investment, at the beginning, on the grounds of cost. Once a line takes off the situation eases, but at initiation they will usually try to side-step the issue. If a supplier is tenacious then they will resort to illusion and sleight of hand. If they have in-house product managers then they will choose one for your line who has neither interests nor time. Otherwise they may pick a salesman at random and call him your product specialist. If you are good at your job they will have walked into a trap because they will have conceded the principle of having a specialist but underestimated your skill in actually making the post work!

The root of this skill will be training, but of a special intensity for the product specialist. In addition to thorough grounding in background, product, market and application, the product specialist needs a very special personal relationship with the manufacturer, and this is most often best achieved by getting the selected individual out of his office and back to your home ground. Back at base you will have the time and opportunity for detailed indoctrination, not only in product, but in manufacturing processes, quality programmes and repair procedures. There he will have the opportunity to meet and to forge relationships with many others in your company from development people right through to shipping staff, sales co-ordinators and service personnel. Done well, these relationships and this type of exposure to your company will allow the development of the vital but elusive loyalty to your company which will make things happen at the dealership.

For all these good things to happen, however, you will need the right individual. Choosing the wrong person can have the diametrically opposite effect. The specialist should be a reasonably good saleman and, if not hugely popular, then at least acceptable to and respected by the sales team. He must be technically competent and a communicator with a relish for detail. The candidate should not be so good or so ambitious, however, that this position represents merely a stepping stone in a corporate career. The training requirements and inculcation are too arduous to be repeated often.

Initially, when sales are sluggish, probably the only means the product specialist will have of judging your company will be by way of relationship, and in those senstive early days, if he's been well poisoned, he can keep things going through rough patches with dealer managers and salespeople. Later, when things warm up and product starts to move, he will hopefully set sales standards that will serve as a beacon for the general sales force.

Initiation, then, is an action programme that follows fast on the heels of contract. It concentrates on focus and on doing a few things but doing them well, and on getting the sales team to taste success as quickly as possible. It will be the starting point for the sacred fundamentals of dealership training and the recruitment of the vital sales specialist, owned by you but paid for by the dealer. And it represents the final and ultimate closing tool for getting a distributor out of an optional frame of mind and into a committed programme to move product.

7

TRAINING

Making Friends

For many understandable but negative reasons, an untrained salesman will die rather than demonstrate a product to an expert sales prospect. His greatest challenge in life as a salesman is probably the fear of rejection, and there is no faster way to be kicked out of a customer's office than to betray an ignorance of the product or its application. A really significant loss of face in this way not only bruises the ego but usually puts a good and dependable customer out of reach for ever. At best, therefore, a poorly trained salesman will simply avoid the product. At worst he will in fact discourage sales, due either to misconception about the product's capabilities or fear of after-sales problems. Salesmen guard their regular customers jealously. These people are a salesman's lifeline, his only real security, a resource which, carefully cultivated, becomes a key factor in his income potential. So a well-trained salesman will naturally favour a product where he feels confident in front of a knowledgeable customer and where he will get the opportunity not only to write orders, but also to develop his reputation with a customer group and lay the groundwork for further business.

Remember the fundamental – that your real competitors are all those other products handled by your distributor and that the biggest and most significant challenge you will have is to get more and more of a distributor's sales time on to your products. Well, one of the keys to succeeding in this goal is training. If a salesman is better versed in the features and benefits of your products than most others, he will reach for them and talk about them as a matter of reflex. If you've told him clearly who most needs the product and where the customer can be found, then your line will be on his mind when setting schedules and journey cycles. With a good training on the product background and its applications, a salesman will be in a much better situation to recognise opportunities for himself and to appreciate the value, or dangers, of any changes that take place in the market. And if you've given him good selling tips and some interesting new techniques, he's going to enjoy getting to customers, testing them, and making some extra commission at the same time.

Out there in the great big ugly world of merchandising, distributor salesmen are not always adequate to the task. Although patterns are changing with the ever-increasing technical sophistication of products, distributor salesmen are not always highly qualified, technically, and often carry little by way of formal sales training. Whatever their level of formal training or qualification, they are first and foremost human beings. Their relationship with you is crucial, and transcends all other price and performance issues. Any opportunity which you take, therefore, to increase their selling skills and add to their professionalism is greatly appreciated, and will invariably be richly rewarded through special affection for you and your company and that valuable extra focus on your products.

So while training is obviously vital to avoid misrepresentation of the product, its prime purpose is as a tool to focus attention and preference on your product line and as a vehicle for establishing good relationships with the dealer salespeople.

Presentations

Initial approaches to any distributor will require good selling skills, and really slick presentations will be very important in stimulating interest in your product and in motivating good distributors to run with your line. This requirement for excellent presentations is an ongoing requirement in international sales, as it is in most selling businesses. The key to a good presentation, however, is to teach. Well-timed humour will, of course, be appreciated, as will orderly deliveries on product features and benefits, competitive summaries, selling tips and so on. But the mark of a really great presentation is when it leaves the audience wiser, in a general sense, than it was before your talk. Naturally they will be wiser on your product, but what will really make the difference to their appreciation, and, vitally, their retention, is when the group learns not only about a new product but about the industry, the background, and the application.

It's nice to finish a presentation knowing that you covered all the bases and that a few of your standard jokes were, in fact, understood and went down well. But what really makes one glow and realise that the result was special is when one or two of the audience come up afterwards and say: 'Wow! I never heard of that use before, I know five people who'll be immediately interested.' Or: 'That's the tenth time I've had surface-mount explained to me but the first time I've understood it!' Guess who's just made a friend!

Since most of our training will be done by way of presentations, it is wise to take a closer look at the basic elements and techniques which make presentations work.

Audience

Assume first, contrary to all appearances, that your audience knows nothing! Trying to check this by way of query is useless. 'OK, before we hit the servos, do most of you understand squirrel cage motors?' Nine times out of ten all the heads nod in the affirmative. Sadly you've lost most of them somewhere between the zoo and their backyard trying to see the connection. But there is no way a salesman is going to admit in front of his boss, or his peers, that he doesn't know his stuff. Also, with overseas sales groups, misunderstandings will occur even with the best interpretation. There will be a small risk that repetition of the basics may offend a few of the gurus, but this is easily countered with a pre-emptive apology at the very beginning: 'OK, I know most of you probably know an awful lot more than

I do about feedback loops, but if you don't mind I will repeat a few of the basics – it really helps me to give a smoother presentation, and some of you may be new to the subject. . .'

Of course there is the real danger that there are one or two listening who are experts, and this could surface as a real embarrassment later in the presentation, usually by way of deliberately awkward questions. Again that is best pre-empted at the very beginning: 'Now I know some of you are real experts here, and I'm only a poor simple salesman. So if you could keep serious technical questions to the very end I would really appreciate it. By the way, if I can't answer them then – I'll certainly get back to you next week. . .' Now anybody trying to bully you after such modesty would only be a cad. It probably won't happen.

Assessment of the audience at the very beginning is important. If there is a heavy management element we will want to pitch our presentation towards those issues which turn them on, such as profitability and fit. We will also need to do a little ego-pumping by alluding respectfully to superiors from time to time during the talk and occasionally soliciting their support for statements of the obvious. This is all part of the closing technique of drawing management into commitment to the project. In some countries, notably Japan, pecking orders are specially sensitive and close attention must be given, during any public address, to paying proper homage to the various elements of management selected for participation.

If there are academics present, they will need to be assuaged with the right amount of technical detail. Sales meetings should not be confused with technical briefings, however. Salesmen and engineering support types don't mix very well. If the product is technically fairly sophisticated, sales training and technical training should be treated as two separate issues and done at different times.

While some presentations may be better than others and more fun, remember that for most attending it's still only part of a job, something they have to get through, another routine, more stuff to be learned – another challenge. Invariably for some it is seen as a downright intrusion, even a waste of time. So don't punish them. Give them breaks for coffee or a smoke, take a decent lunch break, take time to stretch from time to time and generally use any opportunity you get to let them know that you appreciate their sacrifice!

Technique

Anyone involved closely in international sales has to be able to speak well in public, and if these skills don't come naturally then they had better be learned through one of the myriad books or courses on the subject. So we're going to assume that the export sales manager can speak in front of a group without obvious embarrassment, and while not, perhaps, an Il Duce, can hold the attention of an audience and deliver material in an interesting and orderly manner.

Even skilled talkers do, however, need lots of practice when it comes to product presentations. As opposed to welcoming speeches, awards or tributes, product presentations represent work for the audience, not pleasure – and the invariable technical content doesn't help either. So forget those school speeches and glorious moments at your brother's wedding and concentrate on the special challenge of making solid-state voltage regulators interesting for teams of hungover and apathetic salesmen whose only real wish is that you have a massive coronary before the tea break!

The best way to practise is by giving presentations to your peers. They will know the products, often better than you do, and put you to the test. Superiors will accurately simulate the pressures of a group of strange and cynical salesmen, and the natural enmity of some of your competitive associates will duplicate the often hostile atmosphere of a dealer auditorium. In a way it's like practising for the mile by running a marathon and does wonders for one's confidence.

It is definitely bad medicine ever to prepare a presentation by writing it out fully. This is simply rehearsing a negative and practising a fault. Written preparation should be by way of abbreviated notes only. These can be very lengthy at the beginning but should never attain the length of a manuscript. In this way we will be training ourselves, from the very beginning, to speak and not to parrot, and building up the creative reflexes in our brains. As time goes on these notes will become shorter until we need only key headings to keep continuity and avoid serious omissions.

All sorts of studies have been published to confirm what has been obvious to us since kindergarten: we retain a lot more by reading rather than listening, a whole lot more by taking notes, and a vast lot more if we know we're going to have to pass an exam on the subject. So visual aids are a natural choice to help get a point across and also to put a bit of excitement into the session – provided of course that they are clear and exciting. Similarly, typed summaries will tease retention up a few points provided they are interesting and not too complicated. Finally, we can get most of the audience to take notes by threatening them, albeit in a lighthearted way, with a test at the end of the presentation. This can be done inoffensively but effectively by way of competitive quiz, or in the guise of a special award for the best listener. No one wants to make an ass of himself publicly, and even a simple and brief test will ensure that notes are taken; any resistance can be easily overcome with the promise of a few compensatory beers afterwards.

In terms of resistance, one has to be prepared for the disruptives, the bullies. These will be people who resent the presentation in the first place and are anxious to show it. Perhaps they have been used to a competitive product. Maybe they feel they know more than you do and should be teacher rather than pupil. Often they are just young or perverse and like to see a speaker degraded by a blown presentation. These types are rarely absent and can be recognised even at home-office presentations disguised as friends. The technical bullies can be pre-empted by an early admission of apprenticeship by the speaker and an insistence that questions are dealt with at the end of the presentation. The best way to deal with the sadists is to threaten them with involvement. As soon as they are identified, leave the podium and move towards them holding eye contact. Ask for their names and imply that you may want their help with certain queries during your talk. These people usually aren't that bright, don't really know their subject and fear exposure like the undead. Stripped of anonymity or camouflage, they will quickly run for cover!

Physical movement is, in any case, a good idea. Anchoring

oneself to a podium tends to magnify and focus the life forces of the audience on the speaker and leads to tension, perspiration and shaky hands. A reasonable amount of movement relaxes the speaker, keeps the audience awake and frightens the bullies. Movement becomes more important as one moves away from Western culture and addresses audiences in Asia and particularly in Japan.

The Japanese, particularly, live tensely and their lives are full of stress. It is not untypical for a Japanese salesman to be away from home for 270 nights a year, and a terrible price in family life and relaxation is exacted in return for lifelong tenure in a secure company. The guys will use any opportunity they can get to relax, and a sales presentation usually affords them an hour or two of much-needed sleep. We used to take bets during Japanese sales meetings on how long it would take before the first dealer salesman fell asleep. The all-time record was set in Osaka during a product launch when we lost a delegate at the third slide, during the introduction! Their sleeping tendencies are legendary. One learns to look for the warning signs, which, for Japanese, consist of rolling the head two or three times from side to side followed by a collapsing downward motion signalling complete loss of consciousness. Once they are asleep they must be woken very carefully to avoid damaging loss of face, especially company managers. Prevention is the best cure, and an animated, lively presentation with lots of movement and simple relevant humour works very well. Quite honestly, my own presentations in Japan, particularly, have taken on all the appearances of a panto-mime and cause a lot of initial alarm when I bring a manager with me to Japan for the first time. Their faces blanch at the sight of an export manager prancing about miming product applications, labouring simple little jokes and clichés and tirelessly bowing and maintaining eye contact with key players in the audience. The shock quickly dissipates, however, when the audience responds with interest and attention and when key customers later express their appreciation with warmth and with orders.

The Japanese themselves are first to recognise the dangers of lacklustre presentations. Often a wily Japanese distributor will place one or two key regional managers in a conference room during a seminar, armed with cameras. These managers, preten-ding to record an important event, watch carefully for the telltale roll of the head and rush out to take flash photos of anyone they judge to be on the verge of sleep. It works well, since no conference visitor will want to be immortalised in print as a sleeping delegate! By the same token, I have been at conferences where over 60 per cent of the Japanese visitors have actually fallen asleep and have had to remove a drawling, incomprehensible and inanimate speaker to prevent a walk-out of those still conscious.

In fact, good 'theatrical' technique is needed in different degrees for all audiences, East or West – varying only in the degree of its subtlety.

The Pyramid

The Pyramid is a format for product presentation. It is a sacred order, or sequence, for the delivery of information. It applies whether a presentation takes two hours or three minutes. It makes public speaking easier. It cuts down on omissions. The audience will find presentations simple to follow and to retain. It ensures that presentations follow the sales tenet of first creating a need – and then filling it. It anticipates questions, cuts down interruptions and stamps the speaker as a true professional.

In the pyramid we never talk about market without first thoroughly discussing the product. We never discuss our product until we have dealt with the general product area, its background and applications. And we never discuss the product area until we have addressed the general context or need for the product in the first place. If any of these elements is missing, or out of place, then a sales meeting is incomplete and packs less than its fair share of selling punch.

For example, if we're making a presentation on industrial safety glasses we don't even start off talking about glasses, let alone the ones we make. Instead we talk about eye accidents in industry, their frequency, their cost to the victim and the state, the treatments available and so forth. Done properly, this will naturally and clearly highlight the benefits of prevention to both community and individual. From here we lead into general preventative measures available, such as safer machining processes, machine guards, atmospheric filtering and, of course, protective eyeglasses – taking time to throw up the eyeglass as a cost–effective, convenient and easily enforceable method of heightening safety. Now the audience is sold on the idea of protective eyeglasses. Next we discuss the relative merits and the shortcomings of eyeglasses already available on the market. The stage is now set to roll our product on to the stage. As we go through the features of our product the benefits will now register clearly, because everyone understands the background and the needs. The advantages over our competitors will be understood without recourse to negative selling or 'knocking'. The last steps are to tell them where to sell the product, a few selling tips and a good summary to aid in retention. The basic pyramid steps, therefore, are as follows.

INTRODUCTION: A pleasant brief warm–up, where your products are made, who's who, where you fit in, why you're there and perhaps a little humour to show that you're human. This is the time to identify and deal with the gurus and the bullies, to get some chemistry going and to set the stage for tests. This section must be general only and must on no account show or even mention the specific products which you'll deal with. Even a glance at your product is like giving away the punch line and will set the stage for an anticlimax later.

GENERAL INDUSTRY BACKGROUND: Come prepared, know your field, learn some relevant statistics and politely assume they know nothing. This section is used to define needs and, by implication, opportunities. So, for example, if we sell data input services we'll use this section exclusively to talk about data systems, computer systems and the need for speedy and reliable data input. Done well, we will have statistics on the time and cost of data input and the cost of error in feeding information to computers.

GENERAL PRODUCT BACKGROUND: This is where we start to focus on our product area but in a general way, without yet homing in on our own device. In the example above we would talk about the whole spectrum of data input devices, from the commonest keyboards right through optical character recognition, magnetic stripe, smart cards, voice recognition and so on. In this way we have a vital opportunity to highlight the weaknesses of competitive systems but in a seemingly unbiased and professional way. If our products are specifically barcode scanning devices we will still only allude to barcode, in this section, in a general way – but using the opportunity to firmly establish barcode as the system of choice where speed and accuracy are the prime concern.

OUR SPECIFIC PRODUCT: This now becomes the easy bit. The audience have been guided through the industry and tantalised by the scope and opportunity. Weaknesses of competitive input systems have been clearly established and barcode systems have been ingrained. The stage is now set to show where your products score, and to detail features and benefits positively and in a way which shows how your product meets needs established in the previous section. This is where you unveil your scanners and show how they cost less, last longer and do a better job than those of your competitors. In other words, the preceding sections will have identified the needs and you now use the opportunity to show how your product fills these needs.

THE MARKET: If you have followed the previous steps then the market will already have been identified in general terms. Now is the time, however, to spell out very specifically where the product can be sold and to give these outlets a priority rating so that the dealer salespeople know where to head first to get orders. Remember, you want them to taste success as early as possible. Don't tackle the more difficult sectors until you have momentum.

THE SUMMARY: This is where you take the opportunity to go once more through the full sequence but in highlight format, hitting once again the vital bits of each section which are really important to retain.

If you follow these sequences carefully, and attend well to the summary, you will in fact be achieving a dual goal. You will also be subliminally teaching these salespeople how to sell your product and how, themselves, to make a good presentation. In fact, a further element of distributor training will be the education of the product manager, and you will actually need to coach this individual in presentation routines so that he can care for special market segments and also keep the general sales force up to speed on product knowledge.

The pyramid must be applied irrespective of the time available. If time is short, the individual portions of the pyramid are shortened but not dropped. The pyramid can be followed even if only minutes are available, and hotshots will often only give you minutes to make your point. In such a situation it's easy to screw up: 'Hi! I'm from the HotAir Company and we make thermal storage heaters. These heaters use heavy refractory blocks to store offpeak electricity in the form of heat – releasing it into the room during the day. The system is cheaper than oil or gas heating. I know your company doesn't usually sell heaters but we feel they could dovetail well with your national retail effort in Do-It-Yourself. What do you think?'

Of course you've lost the hotshot somewhere between a pottery and a nuclear reactor. If he has any thoughts rushing out the door they'll be of danger, not opportunity. Try this: 'Hi! Winter's almost here and your customers are wondering how they are going to keep themselves warm this year without going bankrupt. They've left it a bit late for oil or gas heating systems which are hell to install. I've got an electric system which is cheap to run, easy to install and could be a major hitter through your retail chain. Got a minute or two?'

Most people involved in sales, or who have been on sales training courses, recognise the pyramid as a series of basic selling techniques which have been enshrined in selling schools now for years. Indeed, it is true that most good courses on selling, communication, debate or public speaking will embody these principles. Yet it is rare to see the pyramid practised correctly. Instead, speakers will start their meetings proudly displaying their new product and so setting themselves up for interruption, misunderstanding and anticlimax as they later try to place it in context. Newcomers to a subject are lost early in the meeting because they are treated like experts. Audiences become cynical and even angry with the presenter because he has forced himself to deal critically and negatively with competitive products late in the presentation, instead of dispatching them indirectly and subtly early in the meeting. The hardiest, who survive the meeting and retain even some of the data, soon lose interest chasing uninterested customer groups and quickly revert to selling other suppliers' tried and proven products within the dealership.

The Product Manager

Remember that if there is a common denominator in successful distributorships it is a highly motivated product manager. No matter how good distributors look on paper and irrespective of their organisational charts, they live in fear and stress in an underworld where principals must be juggled like helium-filled prostitutes and given just enough nutrition to keep them from rioting. The only reliable way to break through this syndrome is to secure their commitment to a product manager. If this is financially unfeasible, then at least agree on a field salesman as product specialist. Once this is agreed, the remaining but simpler task is to steal the nominee's mind and soul. If this is done well, he or she will become your eyes and ears within the dealership and will act for all intents and purposes like an employee, but without the cost. Even later, when business has built to the point where you can afford a national manager, this internal 'mole' will still be vital in accessing the sales force and understanding just what goes on in the dealership. They will identify which salesmen support your line and which oppose; who needs training and who doesn't; who has senior management's ear and who has not; and which of your proposals will be heeded and which will be quietly 'shelved'.

Getting this type of co-operation is not as difficult as it may sound. The key is motivation. While there are a variety of incentives that can be arranged by way of material reward, the very best incentives are training and relationship. Training will give this individual the relaxation and comfort he or she needs with your product to be effective with the distributor sales force, with key customers and with their own management. Effectiveness in their jobs will enhance their career and their earning potential. Over and above pure training, however, you will need that vital emotional and sentimental attachment to your company and its products, and this can only be developed through a special relationship with you, as the teacher, and with your company through experience.

The product manager or specialist must therefore be trained to approximately your own level of competence, not only in product knowledge but in presentation ability and sales skills. This takes a very different type of saturation training and is best accomplished outside of the dealership and back at your base. There also the time can be taken in the evenings, over dinner, in the cafeteria, over a weekend and with the involvement of key and senior people from within your own company, to build the type of relationship discussed.

The Sales Team

The degree to which one can train a sales force will be dictated largely by the time and resources which you have available to do the job. Essential is direct training from your company at the distributor's scheduled national sales meetings or at special meetings arranged for that purpose. Next in order of desirability are actual working sessions with the salespeople in the field. First, hands-on field sales training is worth 1,000 lectures. Second, you will actually be directly helping the salesperson to sell product and make money, a powerful incentive. Last, you get a chance, quietly and over a beer, to establish the key personal relationship that makes the difference. If a dealer salesman works with you, likes you and learns from you, he will naturally want to please you on your next visit and certainly won't forget your products on his calls.

A supplier is not likely to have the resources for significant field-work with dealer salespeople during the early days of building an export business. So the product manager becomes even more vital in filling ongoing training requirements, at least in part. Later, as business builds, product training and field-work with distributor salesmen will be key reasons for investing in overseas territory sales staff.

So, then, the whole process of infiltrating a distributorship and stealing salesmen's time begins with and revolves around product training. It will be the foundation on which relationships are built and fostered and the means for eventually forging dealerships into an extension of your own business.

Good training takes teaching skills and excellent presentation techniques, and needs an individual who studies his audience and stimulates them with a coherent professional presentation which is fun to listen to and easily remembered.

Good distributor training doesn't stop with the next flight out of town but is part of an ongoing process supported, by hook or by crook, from within the dealership.

8

MOTIVATING THE DISTRIBUTOR

It is quite easy in the selling game to get caught up in one's own eloquence and actually becomes a victim of self-hypnosis. We spend so much time romancing the product and and persuading others that we fall into the trap of seeing our distributors as cults, devoted to our product on the grounds of quality, function, leadership, prestige, technology and a host of other abstracts. It is certainly true that these, individually or collectively, are important attributes, and a lot of smart companies, once established in a distribution network, devote a lot of effort to reinforcing such messages with their trading partners.

In proliferous distribution arrangements, trade shows provide an excellent and economical supplement to the management of dealer networks. Here principals can meet large numbers of trading partners in one location, launch new products, do deals and meet key individuals at a fraction of the cost of visiting these people in the marketplace. These venues are also used extensively by established companies to hammer home corporate messages to the trade and to underscore, by imagery, the value of their franchises. The spending and creativity of some of the major pharmaceutical and computer companies at these shows are legendary, with displays covering thousands of square metres, booth staffs of hundreds and after-show extravaganzas that would make Ziegfeld proud!

Yet more money is spent on elaborate corporate brochures and junkets for distributors back at factory headquarters or at exotic vacation spots. These methods can be effective, and even economical, where the primary goal is communication: communicating the launch of a new product or the acquisition of a new technology, widely and quickly; communication to correct a troublesome misconception, say on quality, financial strength or corporate change; or announcing a distribution change, such as a diversification in retail outlets.

History has also proven the power of propaganda – the fact that if you scream the same message loud enough and long enough at the same group, then a certain known percentage will choose to believe. In the same way some distributors will acquire and retain a franchise on the basis of a perceived quality, rather than on the basis of actual financial performance.

But the vast majority of distributors, sooner or later, will evaluate a franchise based on the fundamental motive – profit. And that is the really good news for a fledgeling company trying to build an export business. The big splash or the junket communicates. It also drags along a few of the weaker minds. But this type of extravagant expense is definitely not needed in the early days, when the prime objective is to motivate dealers to work with your line. As the business grows, more money will become available for communication goals and corporate hypnotics. In the beginning, however, you need to spend your bucks where they count – initiating, training and dangling a profit carrot in front of your new distributors!

Pricing

Obviously pricing is a fundamental issue in profits. Equally obviously, pricing is an infinite variable, and volumes can be devoted to this subject alone as it applies to different industries such as textiles, machinery, weapons, electronics, commodity and so on. There are some popular misconceptions:

PRICE LISTS: Net distributor prices should never, ever, be published in the form of price lists. Net prices to different distributors must vary, or else one's approach is naïve, simplistic and does not reflect differing market requirements. If we were to publish these varying net prices then there would be all sorts of different net price lists in circulation. This would be lethal –

invariably someone would goof up and send the wrong list to the wrong person. Secondly, net distributor prices are sensitive and confidential but certain to end up in the hands of a dealer's customer, or competitor, should they actually be published.

Published price lists should exist only in the form of retail price lists or suggested selling prices. Different distributors can calculate their actual net prices by reference to agreed discounts from these retail prices. The price list therefore loses its sensitivity; it means little to a competitor and tells nothing to a customer about the dealer's profits.

Finally, the constant reference to the word 'discount' when discussing prices with your distributor carries a continuous subliminal implication of concession. In fact, in some parts of the globe you just won't get away with a net price list – even if it were desirable. The mentality in many countries in Southern Europe, the Middle East, Africa and Asia is such that a businessman feels castrated if he doesn't squeeze a concession with each order. For them it is a way of life, practically a test of manhood. The constant reference to 'discount' each and every time you ship will satisfy this need and help them to feel that they have haggled successfuly even if, for you, it is only a formality. If you are so foolish as to publish net prices, they will either bleed you to death on every order or else feel cheated and lose interest in the line.

PRICE CONTROL: Control of a distributor's selling prices, in absolute terms, is neither possible nor desirable. We're talking about international markets where the costs of importation. the costs of distribution and the costs of selling vary enormously. An Indian importer may have to pay 60 per cent more import duty than his European counterpart. Japanese main distributors have to cater for the costs of a unique and costly chain of intermediaries and sub-distributors. Distributors in the Philippines have to meet enormous bank charges in raising letters of credit and import permits. Importers in many other countries have to face frightening 'gratuity' costs in order to clear the goods on import or to be considered in competitive tenders.

To many, this point may seem obvious. Yet if I had a dollar for every time I have had to painstakingly explain this point to suppliers I would be a wealthy man. Time after time American companies faint when they compare domestic US prices with actual selling prices in Japan, France or New Zealand, and automatically jump to the conclusion that the distributor is, in American terms, gouging and killing the market. This in fact may well be the case, but can be concluded only after a look at competitive prices and a study of the necessary gross margins in the country in question.

The kind of price control which is practical and effective is in fact an ongoing process of negotiation, concession and counterconcession, where you coax your distributors towards prices which yield good profits while maintaining competitiveness.

In a good, balanced relationship both parties must be willing to keep an open mind. A classic case is where a distributor sacrifices his normal margins during a period of intense competition or when his purchase currency strengthens greatly against the local currency. Naturally, when the heat is off he'll want to compensate himself and reap the rewards of a fat profit margin. Knowing when to let him plunder a little and when to steer him back to more competitive prices and reasonable margins is part and parcel of the thrill and challenge of commercial life. Success depends on being involved, doing the calculations, negotiating, monitoring. There is no room for simplistic rules or attitudes.

Margins

It is accepted that required gross profit margins will vary greatly depending on the industry and circumstances and that there is no way to legislate for these. The point is that, in any case, they have to be satisfactory. A smart dealer will cut lines that take from his bottom line. A stupid one will go bust working on poor profits and be useless anyway. Any dealer will focus most on those lines which contribute greatest to his net profits. Sometimes low-profit high-volume lines will be good for cash-flow, especially in cash businesses. This is really just another way of saying that they are profitable. The essence of holding a distributor's attention is profit, and the ultimate goal should be to make your line one of the top profit-earners with dealers. If this can be done and you can get your line into, say, the top seven profit-makers –

then you're home and dry with your distributors. If you can bring your line to that position with medium-sized international distributors you will join the élite – distributors will kill for your franchise. It will be the proverbial seller's market!

With the exception of the United States, most typical equipment distribution companies will flourish on a gross margin of 40 per cent. They can live on a 30 per cent margin but are usually in trouble on anything less. At initiation, then, a distributor will take your retail or suggested selling prices and apply the discount which you offer – say 40 per cent. A European dealer importing from Asia or America will then add something like 15 per cent for landing costs – depending on shipping costs, duties, insurances and so on. He will then double this landed cost to arrive at his selling price. Although this theoretically yields a 50 per cent gross margin, he knows that he's going to have to do deals and discount regularly and that he must price at this level to have a chance of making an actual gross margin of 40 per cent. The last operation is to convert into his local currency. Using a calculator, you can see that his final price list will be 38 per cent higher than your suggested prices. It is this which blows American or British minds when they forget about the advantages of their own exceptional economies. Even this example is one of the more reasonable cases. The problems really start when they see Japanese price lists with their enormous provisions for 'middlemen'. Often the fastest solution is to ask the affronted party to pay for a steak and a night out in Tokyo and then discuss the matter again in the morning!

So, in the example above, the vital test for your product is that it will compete at a price which will allow the dealer to gross around 40 per cent.

In that the world is not homogeneous, there can be no credible argument for price uniformity from country to country. Therefore there can be no credible argument for uniform discount policies. A uniform discount policy simply implies that you are giving too much profit to distributors in some countries and not enough in others. A uniform discount policy is normally the sign of a lazy approach to territory analysis and it usually has some bad consequences. Typically, many dealers will end up making much bigger profits than the supplier. This, in itself, would not be too bad if the supplier were making good bucks in all his markets. Chances are, however, that in some of the more competitive markets the supplier is being bled for extra discounts because of adverse currencies, competitor dumping and other market adversities. Clearly, then, where the market will permit, a supplier should trim his discounts so as to leave an adequate gross margin, and hence motivation, for his distributor, and at the same time park some extra profits for himself into a reserve account to help in those markets where there is price pressure.

Less experienced international business people often see this policy of varied discounts as robbing Peter to feed Paul and worry that, if discovered, it will be seen as cheating. This is rubbish. First of all, a distributor's prime concern is to make adequate profit. Provided this is happening, you have fulfilled your part of the bargain. If he does discover that bigger discounts are available to other territories, there may be a small diplomatic challenge. A supplier will need to explain to the offended distributor that if he should need similar assistance by way of extra discount, in order to be competitive, it will be available. Furthermore, a supplier's expenses in dealing with different territories are rarely uniform. He will, for example, need sales staff of his own in some territories but not in others. Variations in discount can easily be explained by reference to higher sales expenses in certain countries.

Of course, if a distributor discovers, perhaps through talking to others in the trade, that there is a mother lode of extra discount there for the grabbing, then, being only human, he is bound to have a go at it! It is the task of an international salesman to know his market, to know prevailing prices and to understand his dealer's gross margins in order to negotiate successfully on these pricing issues. And it's also part of the fun!

Incentives

There are other good reasons for manipulating discounts. In the normal course of events a manufacturer will want his distributor to engage in a variety of activities and promotions in order to stimulate business in a territory. Even with good profitability, good training and good product management dealerships are still human organisations and default easily. With the best will in the world they will talk freely of mailing campaigns, special price promotions, advertising campaigns and the like. Sadly, however, many of these programmes fall through the cracks and never see the light of day. The poor distributor has simply too many principals, too many lines, too little time to satisfy all his suppliers – even the good ones. So the overall incentive of profitability, excellent training and first-class product management just aren't good enough, on their own, to ensure that agreed programmes are implemented. The only effective way to make sure they get done is to attach to some or all of them a specific, palpable and attractive incentive that is conditional on implementation of a programme.

There are many ways of doing this: it may be a price reduction to the customer which would be funded equally by the dealer and the supplier; it could be the provision of a number of free samples for trials; it might be sharing the cost of an advertising programme or participating in the costs of an exhibition; sometimes a supplier might push cash towards a sales team's commissions. The ways are endless, but tangible sacrifices by the supplier will ensure that the programme flies.

The extent to which this type of up-front incentive is needed will vary greatly in different countries and cultures. In the more linear-thinking central European countries the business culture prefers more regular discounting and a relatively modest amount of support by way of concession. So this type of expense can normally be catered for in the lower portion of the profit and loss statement under 'sales promotional expense' or similar. In many other countries in Asia and the Middle East, however, little will be achieved by way of special effort without matching contributions from the supplier.

Sure, the arguments against this are endless: 'We give you a damned good margin! As a dealer it's your responsibility to pay for sales promotion!' Or: 'Just what are you supposed to be doing for us anyway? Do you know what it cost to come down on this trip?'

The point is, you lose the war. The best course is to face up to the necessity for this type of incentive and plan for it. And if it is going to be a lot more than a normal provision then it needs to be catered for in the pricing – in other words, in the discounting structure, higher up in the P & L.

Stocking

Perhaps it seems strange to include inventory in a section dealing with dealer motivation. The fact is, however, that inventory is one of the best tools available for galvanising a distributor into action.

A reasonable level of inventory must be agreed at contract. There can be no hard and fast rules to define this. Where a product line is reasonably compact and has good shelf-life and low obsolescence, a level of inventory might be agreed which would ensure that your products would be available to customers ex-stock 98 per cent of the time in a given country. Often, however, products have a high 'custom' element or a range may be extremely diverse, involving, literally, thousands of permutations of product. Expecting a distributor to make all of these available, ex-stock, to his customers just would not be reasonable. In such a case it might be agreed that he would carry sampling level inventory only, and you, as manufacturer, would have to figure out some way of getting merchandise quickly to that dealer to fill larger orders. You might even consider consignment inventory and, later on, a central distribution point under your own control but nearer to the territory.

In other cases where very high-value capital equipment is involved, inventory of any description might be out of the question.

In the majority of cases, however, distributors will end up with a certain inventory which they will regard as both asset and threat. It will be an asset because the inventory is, in fact, the distributor's *raison d'être*. It is his ability to deliver your product quickly to a customer and to collect payment that justifies his very existence. And he will have learned that price is certainly not the only element in being competitive and that delivery and service often count more in securing a market.

The stock will be a threat in that it costs money in tied up capital. And there are always risks of obsolescence and dreaded 'dead stock'.

As a supplier who wants to see his market share grow, you will normally want to see the distributor carry enough inventory to keep the customer happy. This means keeping the salesmen happy too, since there is little more frustrating to a good salesman than to close a sale but be unable to deliver. Smart suppliers also like to keep inventory up for another reason. If they can succeed in 'loading up' a dealer's inventory they know that this will surface as a financial problem for dealer management. Provided that the supplier has protected himself against return of merchandise, the distributor will have no alternative but to pressurise his sales force to move product out to customers and thus offload the stock. This, therefore, is one heck of a way to achieve the goal of having dealer sales staff focus on your products rather than others!

Maintaining pressure on dealer inventories is a valid promotion. Companies often hurt themselves by greatly increasing the efficiency of their deliveries to distributors. This will work well with aggressive professional modern distributors who understand focus, promotion and sales planning and who are not easily diverted from agreed commitments. Sadly, however, these are in the minority, and most distribution companies still operate in the fire-fighting mode. Relieving pressure on their stocks usually also deflates their sales effort.

Of course, overloading inventory is also dangerous. Today, as companies become more progressive with better management information systems and controls, it is less easy to load up inventories – but clever salesmen still find ways. Most frequently a distributor just can't afford to lose a franchise, and a principal will use this fear and force him to reach agreed purchase targets with needless inventory purchases. Last-minute purchase orders at year end, for this purpose, could be called 'franchise fees'.

Often, if purchase controls are slack, a salesman can use a relationship with a product manager – and perhaps some unethical incentives – to slip in some last minute purchase orders. A purchasing manager might be easily manipulated or the victim of well-orchestrated confusion between the sales and purchasing departments in a dealership. Many times distributors just don't know their markets and order crazy quantities on impulse. These stories often have a sad ending. A distributor who never gets to grips with an over-loaded inventory ends up with a heap of obsolete product which will ultimately become a problem for the supplier. Sometimes senseless cycles of year-end loading are established as a pattern, with little result on the marketplace other than a hiatus of orders in the new year to the supplier – and the resultant havoc on his manufacturing planning.

Another problem with inventory loading schemes is that they are like some drugs – one whiff and you are hooked for life. Once a salesman uses December loading to reach his target figures for the year he will find that he must repeat the exercise every year in order to avoid a crash in his sales to the distributor. This is one reason why bonus incentives to international sales staff have to be watched very carefully. There have been notorious cases of regional managers making huge commissions by loading up international territories for a few years. A well-timed change of jobs leaves their successor with the miserable task of correcting the problem while the 'king of the load' goes on to new pastures!

Finally, there are some really oddball ways of pumping up distributor orders. A price increase is, in fact, one of the better 'promotions' open to a supplier when he needs the kiss-of-life on his sales figures. Like any department store sale, dealers will stuff in orders to beat that increase, even if it does not, strictly, make sound financial sense.

The threat of slow deliveries, say over a vacation period, is another good tool for prising off-season orders. In fact any threat to supply, such as a strike, relocation of premises or warehouse fire – real or imaginary – can be used to stimulate orders.

Payment

Many companies see payment as a very separate issue from any sales or marketing considerations. They will usually insist that payment issues are dealt with by other departments, such as accounts or corporate credit control. Often they will posture themselves as worldly and flexible on discount and pricing issues but adamant on rigid adherence to standard payment terms. While keeping to agreed payment terms is important, the imposition of standardised non-negotiable terms does not match commercial reality. Inflexible attitudes here often go back to childhood experience of some senior executive or can be rooted in some work ethic or ethnic trauma. Again one hears the clichés about 'not being in the lending business!' Extending credit to customers is relegated to the area of the unclean, a sort of messy and undesirable personal affair which should be raised only with the plaintiff's bankers or with his family – but definitely not with his supplier!

The really important thing in connection with payment issues is to be paid! The method and the time taken to pay are purely issues of commercial accommodation and should be as flexible and negotiable as possible, within the constraints of security. If payment is handled this way it becomes another valuable tool in building business partnerships and motivating distributors. Seen this way, payment is then just another pricing or discounting issue. If a distributor needs extended payment terms then these should be granted, provided they can be secured. The only remaining issue relates to who should foot the cost of the extended credit, and this will vary depending on the circumstances. Sometimes the supplier may carry the cost, depending on how his accountants view the incremental value of the business. In most situations the distributor can be made to pay for extended credit based on varying his discounts. In fact, during the contract stage with a new dealer, it is always best to ascertain the new dealer's preferred method of payment before discussing discounts. In this way, if he needs abnormal credit it can be funded through his discount structures – and usually without his even realising it!

Once credit terms are agreed they must be strictly enforced. This pattern has to be set from the very beginning, otherwise your new customer will see payment as a monthly chess game where he can massage his cash-flow with every conceivable kind of alibi and obfuscation, conceding payment always at the edge of the abyss and with many extra days to his credit. Although your normal credit terms may be, say, sixty days from invoice for a financially healthy company, it is good practice with a new distributor to insist on tighter protected terms for the first few shipments, even with good financial records. It is simply good medicine and sets the tone for later dealings. If he really wants your line he won't let a cash payment or sight draft stand in his way.

Export credit exposure is a serious issue for all companies and critical for smaller start-up operations. Most governments today underwrite excellent export credit programmes to help beginners. Unfortunately these programmes are often over-looked by larger companies who prefer to 'self-insure', and a credit manager is hired to run the programme. The problem with this approach is that the credit manager is measured on his ability to avoid credit losses. Rather than self-insuring, the pro-gramme really becomes one of minimising and the use of credit as a selling tool goes out the window. To the contrary, the issue of credit becomes a constant abrasive between the controller, the sales department and the distributor – fuelled by obnoxious credit notices, terse warnings and delayed shipments.

The West Germans are an excellent example. Here is a race with an extraordinarily high ethic in regard to prompt payment of bills. Credit is almost a non-issue when trading in Germany. Payment vouchers are passed directly to suppliers' bank accounts. There are no chequebooks as we know them. Bad debts are a rarity except in the case of stupidity or collapse. Yet German exporters are the most creative and flexible when it comes to payment terms with overseas dealers, the loan of demonstration equipment and the placement of consignment stock.

Internal Promotion

An internal promotion is one which stimulates business between the supplier and the distributor without necessarily involving the end customer. We have already touched on internal promotion when we talk about incentivating the dealer by extending his credit, giving special discounts, helping with his advertising costs, contributing to exhibitions, loaning him samples and so forth. All of these should be tied to specific targets. These can be action targets, such as the implementation of certain sales plans, or specific purchase targets. An annual rebate is an excellent way to tie reward to purchase performance. This would be set up so that a distributor would get a retroactive additional discount provided he reached an agreed target for purchases. Again these schemes do have to be watched very carefully, as they are powerful loading mechanisms. The better ones are tied in to agreed selling actions, promotions and even distributor out-sales performance, in order to lessen the risk of overloading, with all its subsequent problems.

Incentive programmes which are aimed at the distributor's sales staff are also very effective. Typically a cash bonus or prize is made available to a group of salespeople within the dealership or to a product manager for reaching certain targets. There are, however, a number of things to watch. For starters, the programme has to be fair, and this is not always easy to achieve. If you set up a sales prize for the best performer, or the best improver, during a certain period – and everyone knows in advance who is going to win – the programme will achieve nothing. In fact it may have a negative effect by irritating some of the sales staff.

If possible, it is good in some way to tie a specific incentive programme for dealer sales staff into overall dealer performance. In this way you don't end up paying out handsome bonus cheques but still end up with a lousy year. This tie-up will ensure that the staff drag their management into the process. By far the best type of award is a trip for the winners which includes a visit to your headquarters. This will give an even greater chance to snatch their brains on your home ground and forge really useful relationships. It can be done via London, Vienna, Bali or Disneyland. The point is to combine a little business with the well-earned pleasure.

These programmes usually don't stand a chance without the support of the distributor management, and this is not always easy. They know that you're trying to steal their salesmen's hearts and time and are probably justifiably fearful of its effects on other lines. So the programme has to be sold diplomatically. The best of all worlds is if you can get the dealer management to contribute as well. This will ensure company-wide support for the programme and serious compliance with its conditions. When people have to pay for something they will always treat it with much more respect!

Cash incentives to distributor staff have to be treated very carefully in order to avoid any connotation of poor ethics or corruption. So these programmes should always have a high profile with the distributor senior management and always be sanctioned in writing.

In any case, provided the basics are in place – profits, training, product management – good cost-effective motivation becomes the routine task in eliciting better performance from a distributor network. There are infinite ways of arranging internal promotions or incentives to give your products an edge over all those other items on the dealer's shelf. Prices, margins, discounts, payment terms and stocking policies are not only basic market considerations but are also powerful and often-overlooked opportunities to spur dealers on to greater efforts.

9

MOTIVATING THE CUSTOMER

Stimulating or motivating customers to buy one's own product is a vast topic, and one which is already very well serviced in the bookstores and libraries of the world. It is a very interesting topic and also very diverse. Effective sales stimulants vary enormously, depending on the product or service being marketed. At one end of the scale there is the heady atmosphere of advertising and promotion of consumer products, where battles are fought daily for precious points in the battle for market share and where staggering sums are expanded in the search for brand recognition. At the other extreme there may be highly specialised or technical products – bimetal motors, thermocouples, conductive gels, sensors, thermal insulants, non-destructive testing devices and the like. Advertising and promotion of technical or highly specialised products is understandably more sober but just as essential as that of the commodity. The requirements are the same: to inform, to compete, to stimulate business, to increase market share, to launch a new concept. Unfortunately highly technical or specialised products tend to be made and sold by highly technical types. These people are not natural supporters of promotion, or even simple salesmanship, and consciously or otherwise allow their innate suspicions to dominate. So the real sales promotional needs tend to get buried in the complex bowels of the product itself.

Bores

International sales managers for companies with a heavy technical emphasis in their products, and, indeed, for many other types
of company, are often easy to recognise and sometimes very
predictable in their approach to working distributors. So predictable, in fact, that some are regarded as bores and their meetings
are usually dreaded. In fact some distributors, rather wisely,
employ specialists to deal with such principals. These guys are
given acceptable titles, such as 'commercial manager', and are
assigned to deal with the monotonous discussions, dinner, entertainment and so on, freeing dealer management to get on with
the job. The routines are always the same and based on a foolish
principle – that you can find out what's going on in a marketplace
by talking to a dealer!

The first discussion, then, will be on the distributor's activities
and, of course, a classic opportunity for the application of the
mushroom treatment. This is not really unfair. The dealer is, in
effect, being asked to audit or appraise himself and will naturally
fantasise and embellish. A skilled dealer will then squeeze hours
of discussion out of product literature. Even an accidental
attempt to discuss serious sales promotion will automatically and
endlessly revert to a polemic on sales literature. The available
literature, brochures and so on will never be adequate, never
enough, never in the right language. Lunch will be followed by a
quick presentation to those in the company chosen, for an hour
anyway, to represent the sales team. This may be followed by a
visit to one or two customers. Then a dinner and a promise of
bigger but unspecified things to come – always of course with
patience and more literature! Somewhere along the line, perhaps
at dinner or lunch, an audience will be contrived with a senior
and genuine manager. He will focus on abstracts, the relationship, corporate structures, patience, promotional 'concepts' and,
of course, literature. Somewhere towards the end of the audience
the visitor will be persuaded of an impending massive, but
unspecified, surge in sales and promotional activity. Despite the
current dismal purchases this great leap forward will bring sales
levels to a new dimension. At the core of this initiative will be
sales literature and a vital financial contribution by the supplier to

its cost. Lastly, there will be a critical need for lower prices in order to survive in the marketplace.

Of course, the poor supplier is so terrified at the spectre of a price reduction that he submits readily to an extortionate contribution to undefined literature costs. He leaves with a mixture of apprehension and excitement, no wiser than when he arrived but poorer to the tune of seveal thousands of dollars which will be quickly set off, by the dealer, against overdue account payments.

This account is no exaggeration. At this very minute, in tens of thousands of offices all over the world, vacuous discussions are being held between suppliers and principals with no structure, no objectives, no plan, no checks and balances. International sales executives are jetting from one Hilton to another reviewing sales figures, lubricating relationships, visiting some stooge customers, guzzling food and, metaphorically and literally, getting themselves screwed.

Plan

The essence of productive and efficient distributor management is an annual specific sales promotional plan. When the selection is done, the contracting, the initiation, the training, and when the various internal motives have been set up, the remaining indispensable link to stealing sales time is the promotional cycle – the annual agreed schedule of promotional activities. Stocks, prices, product management, training, sales technique and so forth have all been discussed and agreed. The remaining dynamic and focus for meetings through the year has to be a selling plan.

Naturally the type of selling plan will vary hugely depending on the product involved and also in its complexity related to the customer base. So a supplier of reflective paints will have to consider many different promotional avenues in order to stimulate business at retail level, through mail order houses, with industrial users and specialty distributors, perhaps government and military purchasing centres and so on. He will therefore have to consider a wide range of promotional devices ranging through elemental sales campaigns, mail-shots, journal advertising, trial offers, specialty exhibitions, etc. Conversely, a manufacturer of expensive recycling plant for local governments has a limited and highly defined customer base and will probably want to limit activities to focused sales calling, lobbying and well-targeted public relations work.

If the steps suggested in this book are followed in building an international business then the task of designing an annual sales promotional plan is easier and lots of fun. To be effective it should also be kept simple. You have defined your final customers and when, where and how they purchase. You have identified and perhaps selected intermediaries such as local retailers, regional wholesalers, sub-dealers and so forth. Working with your distributor, it should be easy to prioritise these groups and rank them according to sales potential. Next, draw up a wish list of good and practical ways of stimulating business with each of these groups, with the respective costs and results which can reasonably and intelligently be expected for each action. What should then follow is a classic negotiation between supplier and distributor, where a balance is struck between what the supplier would like and what the dealer is willing to invest.

Let's take a company which makes splashguards for cash-register and computer keyboards. The supplier will have identified a very large customer base: computer and cash register manufacturers, all the vast numbers of existing users of cash registers and computer terminals with keyboards and a whole bevy of keyboard users in industry and government. All these people need to be reached, in addition to a huge array of decision-makers such as computer system consultants, data processing managers, production planners and managers and so forth. Furthermore, there will be a whole array of intermediaries in the distribution chain who will need stimulation – regional wholesalers, computer hardware retailers, systems integrators and many more. Clearly the splashguard supplier would like his distributor to promote to all these groups, calling on manufacturers, exhibiting to consumers, mailing to retail stores, advertising to systems consultants and so on. Equally clearly, the distributor cannot dedicate the entire resources of his company to this one product. And so a compromise will be negotiated, typically an agreed call schedule to all significant keyboard manufacturers, a mail-shot to graded volume retail outlets, a significant display at one major computer exhibition and one major retail show and a special discount promotion through selected regional hardware distributors backed by trade advertising.

Parity

A successful negotiation on distributor promotional activities hinges very much on effective internal distributor motivation as discussed in the last chapter. It is here that astute pricing, discounting and inventory policies will play a key role in ensuring a satisfactory activity programme on one's products. Provision has to be made, in pricing and discounting, to ensure that the negotiation on the distributor's commitment of resources to your product line is at least perceived as fair and balanced. In other words, concessions must be planned for and given. So the splashguard manufacturer might then agree to give a certain number of sample guards at half price to the distributor so that his salesmen can leave them out for customer evaluation. He might make a specific financial contribution to the two exhibitions and also agree to help staff the exhibition stand during the shows. Again, he might provide the artwork for the mail-shot literature piece free of charge and maybe share the cost of the advertisements.

All these concessions will cost money, and this had better be planned for in the discounting policy well in advance. As previously emphasised, there is no room for simplistic attitudes – although they abound and stem from laziness or naïvety, or both: 'You're getting darned good discount from us – it's YOUR job to fund the advertising and sales promotion!' Or: 'Why don't we give you an extra 10 per cent discount and you can take care of all these costs?'

This approach wins arguments but loses sales, for many reasons already discussed. There is one other, however. Anything involving distributor expense, such as a mailing campaign, advertising shot or exhibition, will have to go through an approval procedure with dealer management. Clearly this whole process will be a lot easier for the sales manager or product manager if they can show that they have wrung concessions from the supplier to support the programme. So supported programmes with palpable on-the-spot contributions get approved and implemented – others starve to death on the drawing-board. Product managers also look a darned sight better to their bosses when they can show the ability to negotiate concessions from suppliers – and anything you can do to further the career and earnings of your product manager will be rewarded handsomely with time and effort.

As stated, the ways and means of promoting products are legion, and lifetime studies have been published on practically every aspect. At the end of the day, however, theory must take a back seat to experience, and one of the earliest priorities in an exporting programme is to test different promotional techniques in various countries and find out which ones work best. There are some universal hard facts and ground rules.

Guidance

Never assume that a dealer knows anything about sales promotion. When this assumption is tactfully implemented you will be rewarded with a close and grateful attention to your suggestions. Understandably, distributors handle too many products to master any. If you deftly probe through all the usual buzzphrase and blurb of mail-shot and 'sales actions' you'll find a willing, if sensitive, pupil. Where this is exceptionally well done the dealer will eventually consider the suggestions as his own and 'adopt' the programme.

Simplify

Keep it simple. Three well-implemented sales campaigns or product promotions bring better results than ten half-hearted attempts from a punch-drunk dealership.

Publish

Plan the programme formally and well in advance with well-published dates and details. There should be no grey areas or open loops. Advertising campaigns, for example, should specify the media, the products and the dates. Sales campaigns should be tied to a specific period. Shows should be scheduled. The final programme needs to be circulated widely within the dealership to get as many people as possible on board and tuned in – and therefore further committing the company to the programme.

Pilot

Major programmes, involving a lot of expense, should be piloted. For example, if, in the medical business, one was contemplating a massive mail-shot to all national general medical practitioners, it would be wise to conduct a trial mailing to a group of doctors in a city suburb first, before committing enormous expense. Such limited trial mailings can be done with non-dedicated general literature and cover letter. This keeps cost down even further. Pilot promotions are a good idea even where there is high confidence in a concept because they can be used to assess likely results. This makes the whole job of predicting and inventory planning a lot easier.

Target

Every programme should have a specific quantified goal. Often this will be a shot in the dark, but without it the return on investment can't be measured. Neither can inventory be planned.

Anti-atrophy

Use the promotional plan as the basis for annual contract renewal and target-setting with the distributor. In fact, as a business with a distributor matures, using the sales plan as an axiomatic backbone in negotiations becomes the only valid remedy against the dreaded 'growth atrophy' which infects all dealers. Growth atrophy arises because of the fundamental difference between dealer and principal. The principal is focused only on one product line whereas the dealer has many. For the principal to enjoy acceptable growth, and the favour of his board of directors, his products must grow at some predetermined rate. The dealer also has a board and also has a growth target. The crucial difference, however, is that, within board strategic limitations, the distributor doesn't care where his growth comes from. Basically, as long as he reaches his target growth at acceptable profit margins and without the loss of a strategic franchise, he couldn't care less whether the growth comes from your fine bone china or Korean machine-moulded crystal.

Now if his planned growth is the same as yours, then there probably won't be a problem. There is often, however, a gulf between the two. Take a Japanese distributor in 1988. With practically zero inflation and with increasing domestic competition from yen-boosted imports and dampened exports, a national distributor will be satisfied with consolidated growth of around 7 to 8 per cent and euphoric with more – say 10 per cent. The supplier will have a different set of rules. For an American company 1988 was seen as a boom year for exports, so an export manager will be thinking of unit volume increases on existing products of, say, 10 per cent by either expanding the market or taking market share on price advantage due to the weak dollar, and also allowing for the inevitable maturity or decline of some products. He will expect a further sales invoice growth of 5 per cent for inflation. He is planning to launch new products during the year which are confidently expected to yield a further 5 per cent minimum. So then his goal is an increase in the region of 20 per cent. If he yields to the distributor's 10 per cent target he faces two problems. First, the deficit of 10 per cent in Japan must be made up from another country or countries. Second, his

Japanese distributor will in effect end up robbing Peter to feed Paul. His purchases will rise 5 per cent because of price increases. Also he will probably find it easy and enjoyable to purchase the new product to the tune of 5 per cent of overall volume. Therefore if he limits purchases growth to 10 per cent he must be doing it at the expense of ignoring existing products with good growth potential. In effect, then, the new product was worthless to the supplier, since its sales to the dealer were at the cost of good established products.

One might argue that a supplier can protect himself against this by carefully forecasting products with a distributor so as to justify, say, a 10 per cent growth in volume purchases of older products. This won't, on its own, work. Simply looking at a forecast will never convince a distributor that it is indeed feasible. The only thing that will persuade a distributor to safely forecast growth is a good solid promotional plan where he can see and feel the ways in which products will be made to grow. The sales promotional plan provides the essential credibility to the forecast. A dealer will stick his neck out and forecast above average growth for your line if, and only if, he is comfortable with the predictions – and there can be no comfort without a plan.

Forecasting Base

Forecasting should be done with the distributor only after reaching agreement on the promotional plan. This point should now be easier to grasp. Once a distributor has signed on to a product promotion programme he will be more confident in making product forecasts and more willing to agree to product sales targets. Once a product sales forecast is agreed, the purchases target from the supplier becomes a logical and non-contentious conclusion.

Of course it is true that purchases commitments can be secured without going through these steps. Many times dealers will commit to purchases targets just to secure a contract. We have talked about such commitments as 'franchise fees'. The trouble with these commitments is that, given freely and cynically, they will be treated equally cynically when they prove too difficult.

They are also a poor basis for a supplier's internal planning. The whole forecasting process can be really credible only when it is substantiated and built on solid product forecasts and these are, in turn, critically linked to specific sales promotional plans.

Down the Line

The best product promotions involve incentives for all the critical parties involved – the ultimate customer, the distributor and the distributor sales staff. Usually all three are critical to the success of a special campaign or promotion. An example would be a mailing campaign on, say, laboratory microscopes. Let's say the mailing is aimed at decision-makers in institutional laboratories such as pathology labs and those in universities, regional technical colleges and so on. The mailing itself will consist of an attractive piece extolling the features and benefits of the product. It will normally include a special price break, trade-in offer or such in order to incentivate the customer to make a purchase decision – or at least to explore one. For a suitable product this type of promotion, on its own, can be quite effective. But the results can be considerably improved by spreading the promotion to the other groups involved – dealer management and the sales force. For instance, the distributor may earn a special once-off discount if he agrees to order extra product so as to be able to respond adequately to the promotion with prompt shipments. Maybe also the dealer will agree to extend the mailing if the supplier provides the mailing pieces, or at least the artwork, free of charge.

Since many of the mailers will arouse interest, but no direct sale, the follow-up by the distributor's sales force in visiting the laboratories mailed is crucial. Here again an incentive to the sales group is suggested – possibly a special extra commission during the period of the promotion, or a sales prize for special achievers.

Finally, if there are intermediaries, such as sub-distributors, in the sales loop they also can be incentivated to take a more active role in the promotion, possibly with a premium discount on the product during the campaign.

It is sometimes argued that the mailing and the price concession to the customer is sufficient and that salesmen and sub-dealers should be thankful enough for the stimulus this gives to sales. This can be true but has to be weighed carefully. If the campaign is highly price-sensitive there can be cases where sub-dealers will accept a drop in margin to help meet customer price targets, and salesmen, too, will often be satisfied with a device which boosts their sales and commissions. This is more common, however, with proven products and proven promotions. A harder sell will usually require sweeteners for salesmen, sub-dealers and retailers. Often, too, distributorships become saturated with promotions from different suppliers and the sales force become snowblind and unresponsive to new deals – again suggesting an incentive. All in all, an incentive which runs deeply through the sales chain gets the best results and does not have to cost an arm and a leg.

Save It

New products are self-promoting. Prices, discounts and other concessions should not be wasted on new products. These should be saved for later, and necessary, kisses of life in the product cycle. The excitement and novelty of a product launch will generate enough enthusiasm and interest in its own right. Stocking orders will be relatively easy and sales should be buoyant during the initial market infill. Special prices, sales prizes or dealer discounts will only cheapen the exercise and undermine confidence in the product's ability to compete.

Matching

Concessions from the supplier should always be at least matched by the distributor. The reasoning here is simple. If one pays for something one treats it with a lot more respect than if it comes free. When a distributor puts hard cash into a programme he's going to make darned sure that it is implemented and implemented well! So share the price cut to the customer with the distributor. Make him print the mailers but give him the printer's artwork free of charge. Go halves with him on the salesmen's commission premium. In this way management will be 100 per cent behind the programme and the whole campaign will get a high profile in the dealership.

Goodwill

Try to measure and put a value on the spin-off from sales promotions. It is clear that most promotions have a far greater impact than the pure direct sales which result from a specific action. There is the considerable advertising value, irrespective of sales. Other products get a boost from the publicity. Presence can be established in an entirely new market. Relationships are consolidated with retailers and sub-dealers. The competition is given a strategic body blow. All these benefits have value. They should be expressed in terms of hard cash. This isn't as difficult as it seems. Estimates can be derived from the cost of achieving these things by other means, such as advertising. Imputing a value like this helps in three ways. First, it helps to sell the programme to dealer management. Second, it allows a more accurate assessment of return on investment for both distributor and supplier. Last, and significantly, many programmes do not live up to expectations in terms of direct sales generated during the promotion. A tangible assessment of all these peripheral but compensatory benefits will help everyone feel a little better about the result and a lot more receptive to subsequent proposals!

Rackets

Watch out for sucker deals, bum steers and lazy options. This may sound coarse, but the life of an international manager at times seems devoted to fighting mythological promotions and useless theories. For example, distributors commit themselves annually to a number of exhibitions. Their next task is to get principals to pay for them. So each trade show or exhibition will

be touted, to each supplier, as though it was exclusively committed for his line and irrelevant to any of the dealer's other
products. Sometimes another supplier may have pledged full
financial support for a special mailing campaign to a target group
which may, conveniently, overlap with your own customer
group. You'll soon find your products slotted into the back page
of the mailing piece – or one of your brochures stuffed in the
same envelope – and a demand for a fat contribution to the
mailing costs. It's not unusual for a dealer to be paid three or four
times for the same mailing, a profitable enterprise in its own
right!

And of course there are those sales managers and product
managers who neither know nor care about the true potential of
different promotional investments. They toss advertising and
literature requirements around like old well-chewed bones, and
no meeting seems complete without a wearying discussion on a
new brochure or an extravagant and dubious advertising shot.
The only way to meet the challenge is to listen, probe the
purposes, draw on experience and tactfully defuse the issue. If it's
a sales manager, or higher, just procrastinate. If it's a product
manager, get him out in the field selling. Chances are he has too
much desk time!

External promotion is, then, our link with end-user activity
and fundamental to our involvement in the process of selling
through a distributorship. It is a vital corollary to an inventory
policy.

A specific sales promotional plan gives us confidence in product out-sales forecasts. This in turn gives us confidence in
purchase commitments. In fact, it can be said that successful
distributor management is directly related to our involvement in
dealer sales activities. A novice focuses only on bullying and
begging at dealer headquarters to pump his factory sales up. A
mature international sales operation focuses on distributor
selling activities and gets progressively closer to the market as
time passes.

The effects of individual product programmes are not solely
linked to the product being promoted. Well-chosen promotions
give a general stimulus to the entire product range because they get
customers, and sales staff, talking and thinking about your products. This spin-off effect is well recognised by office equipment

salesmen when they double the photocopier sales during a promotion on typewriters. Astutely chosen promotions, then, are like key players on a football team. Coaches learned a long time ago that if your three key players are on form, on the day, they will pull the whole team through. The same applies to sales programmes.

A respected international manager will be welcome at distributor headquarters for many reasons. Not least is his role as the honey-bee, travelling from country to country cross-pollinating successful proven ideas in product promotion fron one territory to another.

Finally, and elementally, sales promotion represents one more excellent tool with which to prise more and more of the dealer's sales time out of the general arena and on to a supplier's own products.

10

GROWING

Change

Someone may be reading this book who is already active in
international sales but who needs to change because of frustration with the overall rate of development. Of course there will
have been success stories. No one can claim to have the only
method in building export sales. Some of the successes may have
come by design and some by chance. The frustrations will stem
from serious and inexplicable anomalies in the rates at which
different territories are progressing. There will be the so-called
black-spots on the export map – territories which seem to be full
of opportunity, to have many of the right gauge readings, but
where the supplier 'never seems to have any luck'. Distributors
will be changing too frequently and with a lot of difficulty – legal
wrangles, huge inventory returns, continuity problems in
supply of product and service, and many other ugly consequences of poor selection.

In cases of poor original selection the only real solution is a
strip and rebuild. Essentially one must go back to first principles and reappraise each country all over again as though
starting from scratch. Of course this does not mean that all
existing distributors have to be changed. But a thorough rea-
nalysis will suggest many changes in mechanisms and
partners.

Changes are not inevitable. In fact, as we get better at
selection, we will weed out needless change. For example, many

wsuppliers who do the job thoroughly from the beginning end up ith distribution arrangements which have, quite literally, lasted for generations. Well initiated and well supported, these early associations grow in an upward spiral of mutual support and interdependence. A word of warning, however – eventually the very warmth and trust which characterise these relationships can be mistakenly assumed, in their own right, to be its sustenance. Of course warmth and a grand old relationship, say between the owners of the companies involved, is a great help. Those evenings in the Hof Brauhaus in Munich, the exchanges of children for summer vacations and the fishing trips up to the Adirondacks do, of course, contribute to the success of the relationship – but only in the same sense as a special selling skill or communicative ability. Even if actual genuine friendship develops over the years, the business side of the association will still be judged on the main issues. Is the level of sales acceptable? Is the present distribution arrangement the most profitable way of achieving these sales? Are the profits balanced?

If there is still balance in the relationship, and acceptable performance, then change for the sake of change would be stupid. The role of a well-managed distributor can be stretched and stretched to compete successfully and indefinitely with the alternatives and the problems they carry in cost and limitation in sales coverage.

In the great majority of cases, however, if we are doing the job of analysis and selection correctly, then much of our distribution organisation is consigned to change from the moment it is conceived.

It is axiomatic that, if we have succeeded in avoiding the mushroom treatment and being blindsided by dealers, our first sales will also be our first lessons. And these lessons will suggest changes right from the word 'go'. This does not signal error, but rather knowledge. Nor does it have to imply the rupture of business relationships, only their change. Within any of the dealership agreements we are likely to concoct there are numerous opportunities for change and adaptation. Our distributors can be a party, rather than a threat, to our inevitable chrysalises as we grow our business.

Let's look at some possible changes.

Expanding Territories

A proven distributor, with the capacity to expand, is a tremendous resource. Consider the savings in time and effort on screening, selection, training and so forth if we can succeed in stretching a distributor rather than changing him. There is an old Irish saying that 'the devil you know is better than the devil you don't'! For example, we may have started with independent distributors in New Delhi, Bombay, Calcutta and Madras. The Delhi dealer, however, is far more aggressive, committed and successful than the others. If he's willing to expand his resources then it would seem a good bet to back a winner and collaborate with his expansion. A proven Dutch distributor may request an expansion into Benelux as a whole, provided there is no satisfactory commitment already to distribution in Belgium and Luxemburg. Old colonial alliances are also frequently the basis for expansion of a distributor's territory – for example, many Belgian companies will have affiliates in Zaire, French influence is still useful in parts of North and North West Africa, and many British companies still have clout in Nigeria and various other parts of Africa and the Middle East.

Shrinking Territories

This is a process which is not unlike the distillation of wine or good spirits. As we get closer to the market and expand sales our channels may need to become more capillary, and therefore more complex, in order to reach all our potential customers. This process may outgrow our original distributor, who may not now have the regional strengths needed to increase the sales coverage.

This does not have to spell tragedy for the original distributor. On the one hand he surrenders up territory to other dealers, on the other his business is growing to a point where his smaller rescheduled territory is still profitable and therefore attractive. Try to imagine McDonalds limiting their franchise outlets in any country because the original licensee didn't want to expand! On the contrary, McDonald pioneers in many countries will be eventually happy to split the franchise in order to limit investment requirements.

Focusing the Franchise

Again, as we mature and grow, the entire product range may represent too great a burden for any one distributor, or he may not have the experience or expertise to deal with specialised market segments. Therefore other specialty houses may be added which are better geared to focused sectors. A specialised paint manufacturer might start with one national distributor but end up with a special national wholesaler for retail outlet supply, a separate national distributor for major contract work and a series of independent regional distributors for industrial applications.

Franchise focusing is also a good antidote against growth atrophy, which we discussed in the last chapter. Keeping various segments of your product line within dealerships where there is focus, and appetite, is very helpful in assuring that each product group potential is maximised – rather than throwing them all into one big basket where average growth is the name of the game and individual lines may be under-nurtured.

Another benefit of splitting the franchise, either by specialty or by region, is the healthy competitive atmosphere engendered between associated distributors. If it is well engineered, each distributor will accede to the splitting of the franchise but will be keen to see that his company is perceived as a strong rather than weak cog in the new wheel. This is a wonderful opportunity to be polygamous without sacrificing loyalty.

Gearing Up

Back in the selection days we may have gone to smaller and leaner companies because we needed their appetite or simply because we didn't have the track record or the glitter to attract bigger companies who could have done a better job for us. Now, as the business becomes profitable and assumes a higher profile in the market, there will be a change of heart from the bigger fish and they will start to court the product line. Naturally we will have to apply all the usual assessment criteria and be wary of size for its own sake. Sometimes a bigger company will offer benefits, however, which just can't be ignored. If we have developed strength in the market we will now be in a position to drive a bargain and a distributor contract that would have been out of the question when we were just starting.

We have to fight a tendency to feel guilty about such possibilities. First of all, the change is not inevitable. A really aggressive small distributor, threatened by such a situation, will make the investments necessary to expand his operation and keep the franchise. If he is really very good in his area, either geographically or by specialty, but cannot expand for good reasons – and there are many – then there are ways and means of accommodating that dealer within a new franchise. If your line now has high value and if the original dealer is really good, there won't be a problem in engineering his inclusion in the new arrangement by wringing concessions from the new main dealer. The black widow syndrome is, in its own way, an integral and honourable part of the business scene.

Getting Closer

This is probably the most positive and most satisfying way of developing a distribution system if it can be implemented, where we have already found a really good and highly motivated partner who gets us the national coverage which we require. As with every distributor, he will have his faults and weaknesses. He will obfuscate. We still have to fight for sales time. Product management is distracted with too many other duties. The dealer never orders enough product to support a promotion and inventories always have weaknesses. There are the inevitable gaps in national coverage. On the other hand he holds relatively few other major lines and yours is an important contributor to profits. So you get the time needed with management and the sales force and they are highly receptive to internal and external promotional concepts.

In this case nutrients are suggested – but by way of support rather than change. This is where we decide to invest in time and energy and supply the dealer's shortcomings through our own resources. Later, if the market potential can support the cost, we may actually implant our own support staff in the territory. In the interim, however, we may use our own international sales staff, or if alone our own time, to ramp up distributor training and directly to take care of key market sectors and customer groups. Here the product will still flow through the distributor but we will actually devote some of our own selling time to supporting his staff, or to replacing them as the case may be. We will also pick out the other areas where the distributor is weak and take these tasks on our own shoulders – advertising and promotional planning, government contracts and tenders, national exhibit planning and so forth. There are cases where the supplier actually undertakes control of the distributor's inventory! This is not totally outrageous. From the distributor's angle he gets all this support, on a profitable line, for nix. For this, and for a good relationship, he will be prepared to surrender a little trust! In some cases it is a better option to offer financial support towards the hiring of a special and fully devoted product manager, permanently located at the dealership, rather than endlessly supplying help and support from outside, and fully free. Remember, what comes free isn't always respected.

Direct

We have talked about the maturing of the distribution chain by distillation, the contraction of territories, focusing the distribution and complicating the network with more and more elements. This means that the original distribution partners are being forced to give up exclusivity. Since they will be sacrificing gross margins by way of discounts to intermediaries such as retailers and regional sub-dealers, there will be pressure on their profits. They also vitally realise that they are participating in the black widow ritual and know well that the supplier is lessening his dependence on the original partners. The loss of exclusivity, the erosion of margins and the palpable diminution in the dealer's importance to the supplier will all lead to a natural depletion in motivation. Initially the supplier has to increase his sales and promotional support in order to counteract the fall-off in effort. Progressively, however, he will have to tackle even more expensive supports such as product inventory and service-repair facilities. Specifically he may have to warehouse products himself, within the territory, to ensure that deliveries to customers are satisfactory. He may also need to provide repair facilities, since few dealers, in a fractured network, will be interested in repair work.

This progression in distributor support can build to the point where the principal is devoting so much in sales time and other costly supports to the distributor that he starts to consider the wisdom of more direct involvement in the local national sales operation. This can be put in a variety of ways, but they all amount to the same thing – the supplier wants a share of the local distribution profits. He needs these to fund the ever-increasing and costly support which he has to give to his distribution network in order to reach sales and market share goals.

What is happening in this growth model is the gradual transfer of key sales and marketing activities to the supplier, and he will need a proportionate amount of the local nationally generated profits to fund this increasing involvement.

Ultimately, in this progression, he may end up going direct.

It is hardly necessary to list here all the advantages of going direct if it is financially and strategically desirable. Certainly the benefits are enormous in terms of sales and marketing focus and the total control one can exert over one's destiny. There may be further incentives in the form of strategic concerns such as the protection of market share during adverse trading conditions, temporary sacrifices in anticipation of new product, tactical distraction of competitors, and so on. Equally there are ranges of disincentives which may never be thrown up by financial analysis alone and are not always correctly factored.

Starting with the obvious: many countries may quickly generate figures to support a direct operation profitably but, as potential war zones, represent unacceptable risks. Other countries have trading practices and national standards of integrity which, by some Western standards, would make direct investment a nightmare. More again may be acceptable on an ethical level but have a business and social culture which is so complex and ethnically shocking as to render understanding and control of a business impossible for outsiders. For example, corporate loyalty in Japan makes it very difficult to recruit experienced but trustworthy people. Just the opposite is true in other parts of Asia. Labour laws in some European countries can be financially ruinous to fledgeling companies.

Of course there are ways to counteract these negatives, such as part-ownership and equity stakes that allow us to go some way towards the sort of control that direct operations provide but without the exposure.

Choosing

Expanding or maturing a distribution organisation is essentially a question of getting the best bang for your available selling-cost bucks.

At one end of the supply spectrum we have the total commitment to a sole exclusive national distributor – at the other end we have a direct selling operation. If properly implemented, the first offers the maximum in stability and intermediary commitment, in return for the supreme act of faith. The second offers self-determination and control of destiny, which are the dreams of those consigned to work through distributors.

Some export businesses will never grow beyond the initial flirtation. The dollars will never be there to justify more than a watching brief on overseas business. This does not imply a waste of effort. On the contrary, the very effort was the cheapest way of establishing viability or the lack of it. In other cases export sales will grow vigorously and, sooner or later, a 'critical mass' will be achieved which will suggest a direct selling organisation. It is then that the data base culled from action in the marketplace, rather than theory, becomes crucial in the financial and practical assessment of viability.

Investment decision-making is a very big topic in its own right and is already vastly catered for in library and business school.

For our purpose, however, we can state that the triggers for investment and the commitment of resources, either to prop or to replace a distributor network, should be based on sound financial analysis coupled with a commonsense, pragmatic and often gut input from those on the cutting edge of international sales.

It is a time to involve the bean-counters and the finance boys, because picking one's way through an international consolidated profit and loss, and comparing investment returns, is not a task suited to high-street book-keeping. Neither, on the other hand, should it be dressed in voodoo. Well-chosen resource investment is key and simply needs careful sanity checks from the financial camp.

International operations should be broken out into their own P & L as early as possible. Structuring this P & L is, again, a separate topic and one which requires a lot of common sense and input from the accountants, otherwise silly mistakes will be made from the beginning. Either the international division will be unfairly loaded with overheads and financially strangled at birth, or the reverse – it will be undercharged for true factory and selling costs, profits will be artificially inflated and the ground set for poor investment decisions in the future.

This does not imply that international sales have to be profitable initially, or even comparable with domestic profitability. An investment is involved. And the extra sales generated represent an important contribution to manufacturing volumes which, again, needs to be factored. The goal, however, is to have an agreed profitability plan for international operations and projected out over three to five years.

This 'pro-forma' P & L will kick out a certain projected and agreed figure for selling expenses. This, in turn, can be further divided into home and field selling expenses. These average, or target field selling expenses in the pro-forma P & L can then be compared to the actuals arising in each territory and these comparisons can be used as the basis for decisions on investing more, or less, to support distributors in different territories.

Let's take as an example an international sale division with projected sales, for the coming year, of $10,000,000. It is calculated that total selling costs will be $1,500,000. This breaks down further into 'field costs' of $750,000. Field costs are generally only those direct costs in the territory associated with sales, such as salespersons' salaries, subsistence expenses, travelling costs and local office costs. From this example we can see that the company in question is satisfied, for now, to live with overall field selling expenses which are 7.5 per cent of sales.

Assessing the territories is now easier. Say one of the territories has sales of $1,800,000. Let's also say that the territory is managed for the supplier by only one regional manager, based in Paris, and that his total field costs – the costs of keeping him there – are only $100,000. Then his field costs are only 5.6 per cent of sales and he is clearly a contributor to the agreed bottom line target. Another territory with sales of $1,000,000 may have two guys costing $150,000. At 15 per cent this territory is clearly a drag on international profitability.

If, in the first case, sales were bullish and the prognosis for sales expansion was good, further investment in the territory would be eagerly considered. In the second, sales growth would need to be extraordinary to justify sustaining the investment and keeping both people.

So relatively simple cost ratios, taken from the P & L, can be used as qualifiers for territory investment. Further and deeper P & L and balance sheet analysis will be needed when considering the investment of direct trading operations as opposed to the use of intermediaries.

International sales development through distributors can sometimes seem like an odyssey, an epic journey through the Hadean underworld of distributor and intermediary towards the golden fleece, the nirvana of one's own direct selling organisation. The arguments for taking on intermediaries in the first place are compelling, and they are usually unavoidable in the early phases of business. Even if sales and potential profits ultimately reach levels which will support a direct selling organisation in a country, the process of learning, of getting the feet wet, is most economically implemented by committing initially to intermediaries. Such are the frustrations of dealing with middlemen, however, that the thought of dispensing with them hangs there, before the mind of an export executive, as the eternal goal and can eventually lead to the impairment of judgement.

International sales managers need all their skills to get precisely the right balance between each end of the spectrum and to weigh the motivation of the few against the shoe leather of the many. The key is to judge correctly when the bucks are being spent in really increasing sales and improving profitability – rather than simply counteracting a lacklustre and dispirited sales organisation.

Product Growth

The ways in which experience will influence product development, and how product development programmes should recognise an international element, are major subjects in their own right. But there should be no mystique. These programmes should merely be an extrapolation of what we do in our domestic markets to match our products to the market and to cash in on industry opportunities.

Initially product development will be just simple adaptation of existing domestic product to meet obvious overseas customer needs and regulatory requirements. Of course, sometimes these changes can be complex and costly. In fact sometimes regulatory difficulties can preclude entry into a market altogether. A really relevant example would be the formalities and costs of obtaining approval in the US from the Food and Drugs Administration, where time and expense can be mammoth and prohibitive to many enterprises. On the other hand, international electrical safety standards are gradually homogenising and these are now easier to tackle – and less expensive.

In due course, as international business becomes a more significant element in a corporation's activities, so also will the international product development programme – and the whole international marketing programme in general.

In many cases international departments will have to do an apprenticeship for several years before they begin to carry their own clout in terms of marketing input and product development. One might call this the 'crumb theory' of international business development. This theory consigns export departments to feed on the products which fall from the home base table until such time as the volumes are respectable and a base of influence is established. This isn't always the case, of course. Where manufacturers have a higher degree of confidence or a better corporate stomach for gambling, they may decide to cut corners and invest in special product before going to market. However, this is rarely a smart move without research and, again, the most accurate and economical research is derived from sales activity in the marketplace. So crumb theory is hard to escape!

Expanding our team and resources changes neither the task nor the psychological challenges of doing business through a distribution network. None of the fundamentals change. Nor do we get away from analysis, from working back from the marketplace in choosing mechanisms and distributors, from screening, contracting, initiation or training. All these needs remain – all that changes is the scale and the resources needed to get us closer and closer to the real market.

As business develops and changes we really begin to feel the benefits of our programme, which cuts out a lot of theory and desk work and gets a supplier cracking on the best opportunities within his resources. Right from the beginning the exporter will be working to a simple, logical and sequential plan, where good sound screening techniques early on will save a fortune later in bungled choices and wasted time.

Equally important, when things don't work out we can interpret the reasons easily because we are able to distinguish a genuine marketplace barrier from the more likely cause – dealer malaise. When we do make mistakes, and they are inevitable, we will have a framework for change and fast recovery. Our distributor contracts will provide good escape hatches and our previous selection work will yield an enviable list of sound alternatives for dealing with the same territory.

11

AND MORE BESIDES

This book is about building an international business from scratch, so choosing the starting point was obviously not difficult. Choosing where to finish is not so easy. We have gone into quite some considerable detail on the creation of an international distributor network and its subsequent management – at least in the early days. Naturally management of an international business will become more complex as sales grow and marketing strategies and techniques become more refined. As sales volumes grow, so do the stakes. Relatively small swings in the market will become very important. We will graduate from the early realm of building an export business to managing a mature and significant international business and all that that implies in skill, formal training, knowledge and technique.

The vision

It is not too difficult to visualise, or even to plot the successful development of an international sales operation. It will probably start with a single individual implementing most of the basic steps outlined in this book for growing a business through a network of intermediaries.

Any international activity, in its own right, will develop data on product requirements. But the in-built checks and balances of our system will ensure that the feedback on product requirements is reliable. This will initially signal the necessary changes in product to meet international needs. Eventually, as sales and confidence grow, the international product programme will change from one of mere conformance – crumb theory – to one which sets about filling specific and unique international needs and opportunities.

At various stages confident soundings will trigger further investment in sales staff. These will be deployed on the basis of return on investment and will coincide with the growth, refinement and change of the distribution network. Eventually, in some of the larger markets, we will end up with direct trading subsidiaries supporting multi-faceted local dealer networks or perhaps even going fully direct to end-users.

As the sales staff grows so too will management demands, and a formal sales structure will emerge based on country sales staff, national sales management and international territory management. Performance of the individual territories will be continuously appraised either on the basis of separate cost centres or, at least, on simple field sales cost ratios.

As the business grows the fight for growth and market share becomes more subtle and refined. More and more skill and specialised expertise will be needed in channel selection, product planning, promotional programmes, advertising concepts, launch programmes and so on. So the international department will need to respond with marketing specialists, product management, specialised commercial management and others in development and administration to meet the needs of a progressive business.

So while this book has focused on a very simple and pragmatic approach to the process of getting started in exports, there can be no substitute for the qualified and professional management of the technical, marketing and financial issues as the business develops.

Other Issues

As the business develops, plan to confront at least some of the following:

CURRENCY EXCHANGE: This one is a real hornet's nest!

Most companies will start up billing their customers in the company's own national currency. So a German principle will bill an Australian distributor in Deutschmarks, or an American supplier will invoice a German dealer in US dollars. This may well be one less hassle for the accountants. It may also help the managing director feel a lot more secure about standard profit margins. In these days of wild currency fluctuations, however, it can play havoc with an overseas market. Basically it means that your prices to the dealer are changing practically daily. These changes will find their way into the marketplace and will create swings in demand. Theoretically these swings should even out over time. The supplier, in theory, should learn to live with balancing swings in his sales curve but settle for good averages. In practice, however, price swings are bad for business. In times of uncertainty people have a tendency to batten the hatches and do the minimum until things stabilise. So distributor purchasing managers tend to over-think and under-act when exchange rates are volatile. Good solid promotional planning becomes very difficult when prices are unstable in the marketplace. Finally, manipulation of distributors becomes very difficult when their profit margins are allowed to vary wildly. When a strengthening supplier currency makes their purchases expensive they scream blue murder, develop short sight and palm most of the increases on to the end-user. When the currencies swing the other way, and their purchase prices get lower, one hears only the silence of a house of thieves. Challenged to reduce in-market prices, they will only bleat about the hammering they took in previous months. Of course good distributor management can counteract these tactics – but life certainly gets complicated.

Long-term, therefore, it is better to stabilise the unit volume sales curve by stabilising prices, at least in the key markets. Many European currencies are now reasonably stabilised within the European Monetary System – the EMS – and this tendency should continue with the Single Europe movement. Therefore reasonable stability can be achieved by billing European countries in one, or all, of the EMS currencies. Other currencies to consider, for their individual markets, are the Japanese yen, the Australian dollar, the Singapore dollar, the Hong Kong dollar, the Canadian dollar and, of course, the US dollar. Other countries should probably generally be billed in one or other of these stronger currencies. If there are to be exceptions to this, then various forms of protection will need to be considered such as forward purchase of currencies, guarantees and so on.

Essentially, in deciding to stabilise prices by billing in overseas currencies, a principal is electing to accept fluctuations in profitability in return for stabilised unit volumes. He accepts that the benefits of stability in the marketplaces and enhanced production planning outweigh the inconvenience of a cyclic bottom line. Of course many companies, just like distributors, forget the rationale of these policies and foolishly learn to depend on favourable currency directions. While it is true and understandable that companies can be jeopardised by lethal competition due to adverse currencies, all too often the real cause of danger is poor planning and inadequate provision.

In currency matters the process of decision is far from simple, and every available source of expertise should be tapped. Currency exposures can be successfully hedged and this, in itself, is a highly specialised topic. Overseas manufacture within the sales area offers opportunities to stabilise prices and profitability. Overseas purchases of raw materials offer natural hedges to export sales. Overseas employment, investment and borrowings can all be hedging mechanisms. But these are all complex treasury decisions and best dealt with by professionals.

TREASURY FUNCTION: Exchange exposure is, as mentioned, a major treasury consideration. So also is the whole system in which international investments are made and the way in which financial statements are structured and reported. Depending on international laws and opportunities, profits will be modulated, in one country or another, so as to maximise return and minimise taxes.

TAXES: There will be implications for transfer pricing between a parent and subsidiary – say the prices a supplier in America charges its own sales subsidiary in Germany. On one hand there will be the implications of US laws which guard against the artificial overseas transfer of profits. On the other hand there will be German regulations in respect of minimum profits imputable to German sales operations.

There are the well-publicised tax incentives for manufacture in various overseas countries. And there are the famous labyrinth ways of routing profits, through the Caymans and elsewhere, so as to defer taxes or avoid them altogether.

SUBSIDIARY AND BRANCH OPERATIONS: In their simplest form subsidiaries or branch offices may be needed just to protect the parent company from corporate or employee withholding-tax exposures. In most countries today the mere presence of an employee, say a territory salesman, can constitute a liability on the employer for the employee's taxes. Furthermore, even though all sales may be totally indirect through national importers, and although the supplier may engage in no direct trading, governments may still impute income to the principal and thence taxes! Incorporation or branching may be the only secure protection.

Incorporation is often the only really secure method of protecting registered names and designs.

Later there will be more positive reasons for subsidiaries such as national warehousing, service and repair programmes, active trading within a territory and perhaps eventually local manufacturing ventures.

All such offshore entities carry enormous implications for financial reports and accounting, budgeting, treasury and taxation issues.

REGIONAL INVENTORY: We've looked at reasons why a supplier may need to put stock of product into a territory. Most typically this arises either when distribution networks become so fractured that many of the constituent dealers lose interest in adequate stocking, or when the product line is so diverse as to make it financially impractical for dealers to carry adequate stocks of all items. Giving dealers easier access to product is a service which costs money. Suppliers often mistakenly absorb these costs fully into their own sales overhead. In fact, most distributors will be willing to pay a premium for product where they are relieved of inventory worries but can provide an even better service to the customer – so good regional stocking schemes can be self financing.

Never forget, however, the importance of distributor inventory as an internal stimulus to sales activity. An unnecessary regional supplier's warehouse can also be the fastest way to take the steam out of a sales programme!

EQUITY INVESTMENT: One of the best antidotes available

for dealer blindsiding and mushroom treatment is participation in the ownership of the company. A significant equity stake in a distributor's business will normally imply board participation. This not only yields a certain control over the direction of the distribution company but, perhaps more important, yields information. Armed with facts rather than suspicions, a supplier can devote all his energies to marketing and sales considerations rather than to wasteful intrigues associated with culling the truth from independent dealers.

This strategy can progress to the point where a principal owns the controlling equity but allows local national management to retain a significant shareholding. This arrangement can be seen as tantamount to a direct national sales effort but without the routine hassle of running a local sales subsidiary. One gets the near equivalent in terms of control but without all the administrative complication. I recently heard a Danish manufacturer summarise his faith in this system very well, when he said that the only way to sleep at night was to cut international distribution managers in on the action by sharing independent sales companies with them in this way. He felt that they then 'worked like dogs to get rich but took care of all the hassle'.

In many countries it is just too darned difficult or even dangerous to consider operating a subsidiary because of local regulations, local 'gratuity' practices or even the national security situation. Here again, an arm's-length equity participation may be a safe way to effect some useful control over local distribution issues without becoming entangled.

Dealers, as we have noted, do worry about the 'black widow' syndrome. Therefore any move by a supplier towards direct selling operations in any country, however justified, could cause some good dealers in other countries to panic and lose confidence and motivation. Equity participation in independent national sales companies can be kept reasonably confidential, and so a supplier can avoid sending the wrong signals to his distributor network.

And so, as the business grows and becomes complex, more and more commercial issues will come into play such as acquisition, merger and joint venture. These moves will sometimes be suggested to resolve distribution issues or to get access to certain markets. At other times they will represent the most efficient way to expand the product range – a move which might be needed to increase profitability by improving selling cost recovery.

These are all flavours of external issues. But there are many other internal challenges also within a company growing an international business. They are not simple and cannot be easily summarised. In fact, they qualify for full-length treatment, else-where, and in their own right.

Distributor Communications

This is a very important issue in the control of distributors and also has huge implications in the motivation and successful utili-sation of one's own international sales team and in factory control.

We must always remember that the distributor assumes a divine right to lie, or at the very least to conceal the truth, in order to protect his franchise. The only people in any position to check the facts or to know the real situation are the supplier's international sales staff – at first the international manager, and later the international regional salesmen as they are recruited. A smart distributor will therefore have it as one of his earliest goals to undermine and circumvent the international sales staff in any and every conceivable way.

The first trick will be to work very hard at cementing a personal relationship with the chief executive of the principal's company – or the owners, as the case may be. They will go to any lengths to get the international sales manager's boss on his own and to seduce him with lavish entertainment and highly person-alised relationships. Time will also be taken to undermine the international manager. Sometimes subtle, there will be condem-nation by faint praise or by omitting any reference to him during any serious discussions. Later they will hint at immaturity and, in the worse cases, at impropriety, loose sexual behaviour and cheating. As time goes on, and if the unfortunate manager survives these initial attacks, they will insist on communicating directly with the president and frequently omit to even copy the hapless sales manager.

The goal always is to practically neuter the sales manager so that in the inevitable event of a row, a change or a termination they will be able to divide – and thus to conquer.

It is not always easy to counter these strategies. A new international sales manager in a fledgeling export company may not yet enjoy a whole lot of confidence from the top, and his boss may feel more secure with direct lines to the distributors. Other suppliers have owners who are easily flattered by attention from wealthy overseas businessmen. Where a sales manager cannot get support from his bosses in stamping out these practices, he has no option but to revert to painful Pavlovian techniques. Here he sets up a feedback loop so that each time the dealer plays dirty he inflicts pain on the dealer. There are endless ways to do this – delayed credits, changes in payment terms, delayed shipments, withdrawn promotional support and so on. Although the stimulus must appear to be unconnected, the dealer will soon get the message. But the international manager must stay vigilant, as dealers rarely surrender this practice, they merely become more covert!

A victorious sales manager will later find the dealers attempting these tricks with his own regional salesmen. Here the best solution is to insist on linear communication through the international organisation and to support this by loyalty to one's own troops and by deferring to them always, at least in front of the distributors.

People

Recruiting people for international sales positions is a real challenge, particularly in the early stages when building up territory staff. These people will be working largely autonomously and at enormous distances from base. They need to be very versatile in their skills. Some days they will be working in the field with distributor sales staff on customer calls. For this they will need to be good front-line salesmen and have the personality to forge relationships with dealer salesmen. On other days they will be haggling with fat cats at distributor senior management level and need the maturity and negotiating skills to deal effectively with these people. If one hires a straight sales manager the chances are that he's at a stage in his career where he needs the big desks, the maps and the secretaries. He won't be able to relate well either to customer or to dealer sales representatives. On the other hand a good rookie who works wonders with end-users and who can relate like a brother to dealer salesmen will be slaughtered by seasoned proprietors and managers of distribution companies. Nowhere are these problems more compounded than in Japan, where a rigid seniority system makes such 'class flexibility' a virtual impossibility.

Therefore one has to find a rare hybrid, one with the experience and maturity of a sales manager but who is willing to roll up his sleeves and mix in with the plebs. One who understands promotion and incentive but who is willing to do his cerebral marketing on his feet. One who can take the autonomy and lack of supervision without an agoraphobic collapse but who is essentially honest and who can motivate himself to work fairly.

These features are not easy to find in any one individual. I often think that early team members in a growing international business need to be a little mad to cope with the confusion in the career pattern, the autonomy and isolation, the flexibility of their roles and the domestic and personal stress of a life on the road. Take an example:

An international salesman might fly early Monday morning to Oslo to catch his distributor's sales team for a presentation on a new product. After lunch he will have detailed discussions with the product manager on sales plans for the coming year. There will be a session with the advertising manager, the purchasing manager and also the repair department. In the late afternoon he will begin his final negotiations with the managing director on an agreed target of outsales and purchases for the new year. They will also discuss and argue key issues such as regional sales coverage, staff training and turnover, frictions within the national distribution framework, payment and credit topics and lots more. Dinner may be followed by a late flight to Stockholm so as to be ready first thing in the morning for another general product presentation during a valuable slot in their February sales meeting. This will be followed by more general business meetings and perhaps a visit to some key government decision makers. Dinner with management that evening in Stockholm.

An early Wednesday flight to Helsinki in time to participate at a special launching seminar for a new product. If the peripheral meetings can be tied up smoothly he may catch the last flight to Copenhagen, so that all day Thursday can be devoted to meetings with his Danish importer, with the usual socials in the evening. On Friday he will contrive to call perhaps on his Belgian exclusive distributor en route to London.

Monday to Thursday of the following week will be spent in office duties, follow-up to his trip, reports and preparation for his Friday departure to Sydney for similar new year implementation meetings with key dealers in South Pacific and South East Asia. He will leave on Friday, to the detriment of his family and his golf game, but so as to arrive in Sydney with time to rest on Sunday before a strenuous week visiting distributors in New South Wales, Queensland, Victoria, South Australia and perhaps Perth. Each of these meetings will be characterised by the challenge of selling at presentations, consolidating relationships with key sales staff and product management, and mortal combat with dealer management on vital commitments for the coming year.

Auckland might be omitted on this trip. Instead the weekend will be used to travel to Singapore, which will be used as a base to conduct a seminar and individual meetings with selected distributors from the South East Asia region. So key individuals from companies in the Philippines, Indonesia, Thailand, Malaysia, Pakistan and India and others will be induced to travel to Singapore in order to achieve crucial objectives at the start of the year. Visits to each of these countries will be scheduled later in the year in order to work the national sales teams and to conduct important territory work.

On then to Hong Kong, where a similar exercise will be conducted for distributors in the north-east Asian region – Taiwan, Korea, China and, of course, Hong Kong itself. A late Friday flight will see the sales executive back in London on Saturday morning. He will be zomboid over the weekend with fatigue and jet-lag. Essentially, then, he will have enjoyed no family life for three weekends and little for the month in general. Yet on Monday he will be back in the office planning a trip to seven cities in Japan for the second week in March, coming back via Hannover in order to spend a week at a vast and critical electronics fair!

So these people are hard to find and difficult and costly to replace once trained. Their selection, training and management is, again, a separate story. Suffice it to say, for now, that the process of selection and management is a specific and skilful programme. So also is the process of evaluation and reward so that these crazy hybrid people will be prepared to settle for a lifetime career in the lonely, fatiguing, responsible chameleon world of international trading.

Home Office Challenges

It would be nice if all the energy, all the sales and marketing skills, of the international manager could at least be focused externally on the main target – distributors and end-users all over the world. Unfortunately this is not the case, and it is a fact that a surprisingly large amount of selling and communicative ability has to be directed internally and at those who are, on paper, at least, on the same team.

It just would not be reasonable to expect most people on the shop floor or in factory supervision to be naturally *au fait* with the cut and thrust of competition in overseas markets. Their sympathy with difficulties in exporting must be won and not expected as a right. So they will need to be told about overseas price issues. They will need to be shown competitive product and to see fairly how it compares with theirs. The awesome differences in wealth, technology and consumer traditions in different countries need elaboration so that they can understand seemingly irrational patterns in overseas sales. Swings in export sales curves need to be explained, and also the implications of wars, tensions, international trade disputes, see-saw currency exchange rates, inflation and a host of other factors which, one way or another, affect their lives. Mind you, even the best communication programmes won't catch everything. A French factory worker is never going to understand American tastes in food. A British workforce will never grasp why electric kettles are not popular in the United States. Can one really expect a German worker to understand an inflation rate of 800 per cent per year? Can a foreman in a Swiss chocolate factory really grasp an annual bank interest rate of 65 per cent? To a certain extent, therefore, the international department will always wear horns to many back at base. The trick is to minimise the misunderstandings, and no opportunity for presentation or audio-visual explanation should be overlooked. Having distributors come to the factory and meet the staff is a great help – but these visits have to be very carefully controlled and orchestrated to avoid diplomatic incidents and also political conniving on the dealer's part.

Shipping staff and export clerks naturally require special attention. The technical requirements in dealing with export documentation, freighting, routing, insurance, import and export laws and restrictions, monetary instruments and bank documents, invoicing, tariffs, declarations – and much, much more – are considerable. Specialised training is clearly essential. This training, however, will never be complete until the key export sales co-ordinator gets the opportunity to travel and meet his counterparts in various countries. Even then export staff will probably never fully accept the absurd documentation requirements of many overseas governments and their perverse punishment of minor documentary errors or omissions. Just how will you ever convince an export clerk in Shannon that an invoice error could cost the importer his life? Yet I heard of an international manager who was a formal guest at a mass execution of business proprietors convicted of corruption.

On the positive side, a well-trained export co-ordinator can be worth his weight in gold in consolidating distributor relationships and in selling through a company to its customers.

One also has to do battle with the accountants and financial controllers. These people, quite naturally, see life largely in terms of financial checks and balances. Their foremost concerns are to know what is happening, to capture all costs, to protect against surprises. This obsession with identification and collection of costs rears its head in many ways. They like to minimise and simplify budgetary and reporting channels. They prefer uniform expense reports and the minimum of budgetary account numbers. They like to see salaries and such paid at consistent times and in uniform ways. They love uniform discount structures and consistent invoicing practices. All this doesn't mean that they have to be inflexible or obstructive. It's just simply that they default, all the time, to harmonisation as a golden cow of protection. And of course this can make life tough for an international sales manager.

He needs flexibility in discounts and prices; his priority is to locate people based on territory needs rather than administration convenience; his ability to recruit good international staff will depend on his flexibility in reward packages and incentives and creative ways of maximising net earnings for his team; and his budgetary structures will reflect his needs to control teams of individuals and external spending associated with international sales activities.

To be successful, then, with the financial gurus, an international manager will need to focus on understanding their fears and in collaboration and consultation with these groups so as to induce their treasured 'comfort' with the international environment.

Domestic engineering groups can be notoriously chauvinistic and professionally jealous – the old and famous 'it wasn't invented here' syndrome. Getting realistic competitive analyses from these groups can be a real challenge, since it is perceived as a sort of self-audit on their creativity. The response of the American auto industry to the Japanese challenge must be the supreme illustration. Relatively autonomous European subsidiaries of American companies had produced competitive designs in compact and fuel-efficient cars years before their US counterparts reacted adequately. The top brass in the US realised this but seemed unable to swing the engineering groups to a fast enough response. Unfortunately it is very difficult to expose a technical group which has become resistant to change. Their technical smokescreens can faze a corporate gladiator and it often takes a successful thrust from the competition to back them down. Engineering groups must be led to feel that they 'own' part of the international programme, and this has to be achieved by structuring responsibilities in international product development and by the association of security in their domestic market with progress in the international one.

A supplier company's domestic sales team is another political tinder-box. If an international department is having any success this usually means pretty fancy annual percentage increases during the early days. This quickly generates a primadonna perception within the company which is bound to cause resentment within the domestic sales group, where relatively conservative increases are hard-won. Left untreated, this attitude will harden to a belief that the international section is, in reality, responsible for their difficulties by over-pressurising engineering and production groups and starving them of good competitive product.

Sales teams, by definition, tend to be competitive, tribal and polarised, and tensions between domestic and export sales teams are the most difficult to resolve. Joint sales meetings and campus-style gatherings are mostly futile. I have seen fights erupting at well-intentioned games of volleyball between mature men in their thirties and forties.

Often the only solution is to minimise contact between the teams and concentrate one's energies in politically counteracting any dangerous side-effects within the company. Usually the best ploy is to engineer the maximum contact between the factory staff and the international sales team, who are masters of manipulation and motivation in their own right.

Finally, one has to deal with management and one's own bosses. A lucky international manager will have a boss who has served his time overseas and knows the ropes of international business. Often, however, company presidents or managing directors only superficially understand the vast contrasts in conditions and practices between one country and another. Even after occasional trips overseas, and usually to the safer spots, they quickly revert to a planet called 'Home' where prices and discounts are uniform, where there are no boundaries and where there is no commercial culture shock. Since their time is at a premium, one has to be especially clever in finding ways of preventing them from reverting to misunderstandings and even the downright simplistic.

A regular and planned programme of communication and motivation of all the internal groups is essential. Where the information is *ad hoc*, accidental or non-existent there will be suspicion, reticence and even obstruction. Feuds will develop between domestic and export shipping groups. Accountants will view international pricing strategies as questionable and even underhand. Engineering projects for export product will be relegated in priority. Exports will be perceived as an unwarranted primadonna and a whole viral strain of political enemies will permeate the corporation.

On the other hand, planned briefing of the various groups, on a need-to-know basis, defuses suspicion and will help develop a real sense of teamwork throughout the whole company. Furthermore, a specific information programme is a whole lot more efficient. Probing for unspoken objections and teasing out obstructive corporate enemies is a frustrating and time-consuming task. Communication is the fastest and best inoculation against hidden resistance and mistrust.

In this closing chapter we've opened a whole new file on other topics which need to be addressed, sooner or later, in a successful international sales operation. Some of these issues are clearly quite complex and will need special skills. But they should not be alarming. These specialities and skills can be found when the time comes and as the business grows.

Growth will begin with a grasp of the fundamentals in dealing with intermediaries – balance, fairness, data, recognising the enemy.

Our analysis phase is a pragmatic action programme to get data fast and to plan a campaign.

We figure our intermediary mechanisms by working back from reality, from the marketplace.

We select by using the tricks of check and balances.

When we contract it is practical and without delusion and we use a specific initiation phase as a closing tool.

We recognise training as a fundamental which separates us from the other mobs clawing at dealers' resources.

Once we have our system in place we move in with planned programmes of internal incentivation and market promotion.

If we keep our eye on the fundamentals then the growing and the peripherals will take care of themselves, logically and at the right time.

QUICK REFERENCE

This book was not primarily intended as a text, and lists and tabulations were deliberately avoided. However, since there's nothing else available on middlemen, it just might find its way into the classroom. And who knows when a harried international salesman might need a quick refresher? Finally, the publisher insisted! So, herewith a memory tickler:

Fundamentals

- Profits for both parties
- The real fight is for dealer selling time
- All the dealer's other lines are your competitors
- A distributor knows he may outgrow his usefulness
- A supplier's ignorance is a distributor's protection
- The facts of life are tough but understood by all

Analysis

- A day in the field is worth a hundred at the desk
- Learning really starts with selling
- Territories can be quickly shuffled in priority

- Intermediaries are shaped by their environment
- Don't depend on distributors for logic or reason
- Intelligence is often no substitute for action
- Data is certainly no substitute for an order. Read sparingly
- If you want to know about trenches – talk to troops
- Only talk to troops who've been in trenches

Mechanisms

- Consistency in channels usually means ignorance

   The channel choices:

   Sole national exclusive distributor
   Multiple national distributors
   Multiple regional-exclusive distributors
   Multiple national product-exclusive distributors
   National distributor with regional sub-distributors
   National distributor with regional tied direct importers
   Commission agent/manufacturer's representative
   Trading subsidiaries, partners, joint ventures

   A shorter list:

   Sole national exclusive
   Multiple national product-exclusive
   Multiple regional-exclusive
   National distributor with regional sub-distributors
   Commission agent

- Customers are end-users and anyone else who needs persuasion
- Choose distributors by working back from customers
- Distributors will do whatever is necessary to secure a franchise
- Work backwards. Ask What, Why, How, When, Where and Who:

   What are the customers' needs and how do your products compare?
   Why does he buy? What are the triggers?

How is an order generated – what are the steps?
When? Selling cycles and stocking needs
Where do the customers shop right now?
Who? Poll customers to shortlist good dealers

- Shortcuts are tempting, but expensive in the long run

Selection

- Vultures are professional line-collectors – all talk, no action
- Talkers are hard to resist when you need the orders
- Treat distributors like murder suspects and crosscheck data
- Verification – an internal and external audit of the distributor
- The first thing a dealer will buy from you is time
- Often distributors want the franchise for the wrong reasons
- Mistakes in selection can be very expensive
- In the early days, small and hungry dealers are usually best
- The advantages of large dealer cooperatives are often illusory

Contracting

- Initial enthusiasm from a distributor is purely a reflex
- The old national emporia are dead. Dealers today focus.
- Attracting dealers takes all the best selling skills
- Never appear to deal from a position of weakness
- Dress the part
- Prepare your pitch and pre-empt distributor fears
- Contracts are one of the most overrated instruments of business
- Contracts are really only useful on termination

The contract:

Performance – ballpark expected performance levels
Activities – define in detail what the dealer is expected to do
Launching – what is needed to kick the product off?
Inventories – clarify the stocking policies
Personnel – what people is the distributor committing to you?

Training – access to his staff, in-house and in the field
Information – data needed to avoid mushrooming
Exclusivity – how many eggs will be put in which baskets?
Territory – where does the contract apply?
Product – what items are involved, now and in the future?
Sub-distribution – ensure a veto in channel selection
Pricing – protecting both parties' margins against the unexpected
Payment – no ticket – no laundry!
Returns – ensuring a sale is always a sale
Period – how long does the contract run and when can it be ended?
Changes – protection against the unknown
Market development – protection against abstracts

- At least appear to be fair

Initiation

- After contract a high-voltage kickstart is still vital
- The deal isn't closed until the action starts
- Serve the best wine first and wean a dealer with success
- Don't give dealers bad habits with early concessions
- Go for quality, not quantity, in supportive material
- Invest some bucks in efficiently announcing your existence
- Alternatively, you may need to creep up on your competitors
- Good training is a gift that steals a salesman's heart
- Get that key mole working for you within the dealership

Training

- We need to learn good professional presentation skills
- The key to a good presentation is to teach
- Teaching is the vehicle for relationships with dealer sales staff
- Assess your audience, tune your presentation and prepare defences
- **The Pyramid:** A sacred sequence for a product presentation:

Introduction – a pleasant warm up
General industry background – where does the product apply?
General product background – what fills the needs at present?
Our specific product – how does our product compete?
The market – where it can be sold
The summary – one more time but briefly and with punch

- Our inside Man Friday needs training to full supplier proficiency
- Better training involves rehearsals and field work

Motivating the Distributor

- Never publish net distributor prices
- Forget simplistic notions of price control
- The goal is to make your line a top profit earner for the dealer
- Most dealers need incentives to put extra effort on your line
- Upward pressure on stocks can galvanise selling activity
- Credit and payment are really opportunities, not problems
- Internal incentives can give your products the edge

Motivating the Customer

- Distributors are fed up with visits from junketing idiots
- Efficient distributor management means an annual sales plan
- The supplier's and the dealer's efforts must be matched
- Don't take distributors' promotional skills for granted
- Quality in promotions counts more than quantity
- Communicate promotions throughout the dealership well in advance
- Do a trial run before committing to a major programme
- Make sure a promotion has specific quantitative targets
- A promotional plan gives a distributor confidence in growth
- A promotional plan makes forecasting, and commitment, easier

- Make sure all parties in the selling chain are incentivated
- Don't waste concessions on new products
- Nothing focuses the mind like money. Get a dealer to invest.
- Measure and publish the spin-offs from promotions
- Fight tired old promotions and hazy demands for financial support

Growing

- Distribution networks are consigned to change from inception

    Expanding the territories of good proven distributors
    Concentrating more dealers in the same territory
    Allocating different products to specialised distributors
    Upgrading to stronger distributors with bigger resources
- As sales grow we get more access and control
- Critical mass – enough sales to do it ourselves!
- Changes are dictated by return on investment
- Products change to match the market
- Products evolve to meet opportunities

And More Besides

- **Other Issues:**

    Currency rates. Controlling their impact
    Treasury function in managing cash
    Taxation and exposures
    Subsidiary and branch operations as we develop
    Regional inventory to enhance customer service
    Equity investment in distribution for data and control

- Distributors see suppliers' sales people as asset and threat
- Good international staff are flexible, autonomous hybrids
- Fight home-office mistrust with communication